# Curiously Strong:
## A Female Fighter Pilot's Personal Story of Developing Strength

### By Priscilla Giddings
#### Powerlifter • Pilot • Politician

 Publish

Curiously Strong: A Female Fighter Pilot's Personal Story of Developing Strength
Copyright 2018 by Priscilla Giddings

 **Publish**

WIPublish
A Division of Women Ignite International, Boise, ID
www.womenigniteinternational.com

Printed in the United States of America

# Table of Contents

## *Dedication*

*To a world full of curiously strong women,
with special appreciation for my mother, grandmothers, and great-grandmothers who instilled their strength in me,*

*And for my daughter, that she would walk in the legacy of her grandmothers.*

Curiously Strong

## *Foreword*

I hadn't spoken to Priscilla in a while. A long while. But that didn't matter. As soon as she asked me to edit her book, I jumped at the chance to participate in her life in this significant way.

Priscilla is one of those people you can count on to be the same person you knew "back when," no matter how long ago that was. Even though we haven't actually seen each other in ten years, not much has really changed between us. We are comrades, in the sense that we have weathered a significant experience together and have both been beaten by and triumphant over that experience.

The four years I spent daily with Priscilla at the Air Force Academy, sneaking the runners' leftovers or attempting to squat as much as her, was a four-year midrash between us young idealistic women on how we ought to live our lives. And so this collaboration between us on her book is yet again stimulating in the fact that Priscilla challenges a person, me actually, to strive for that dream hidden deep down, that dream that we are significant players in our own spheres of influence.

To this day when I go shopping, I will spot something and think, oh that's so Priscilla, because although Priscilla has grown up, Priscilla is still the same. She is still that same small town, down home, build-my-own-house, sew-my-own-place-mats, and shoot-my-own-dinner type of girl. She's still that I-can-do-one-more-rep, put-another-two-and-a-half-pounds on-the-bar, just-five-more-minutes-of-running type of girl. She is still expecting to do her best and in doing so she holds the ones around her to a higher level of excellence and integrity.

What I hadn't known about Priscilla was exactly how pilot training was for her. See I chickened out—well, really, I have no interest in aircraft which is funny coming from an Air Force vet—and there was no way I could have done pilot training and have survived to have a coherent thought in my head ever again. But Priscilla has grit and drive. What has struck me most about this experience of delving into her post-Academy military experiences is that Priscilla has not compromised her own identity in the pursuit of her successes.

As you read this you will see her poise in the face of some serious adversity. Pilot training and piloting in the Air Force is some pretty serious stuff. The Academy basically spends four years preparing you for the grueling intensity of it, but nothing really compares to the experience itself. Around 3% of the Air Force is pilots and of those 3% only 5% are women and of those women, few are fighter pilots and even fewer still are A-10 pilots. To say Priscilla is the best-of-the-best regardless of her gender is to state a pure fact.

But what is most astounding to me is that everything she has done in her life, from breaking world records as a teen to saving lives in Afghanistan, has led her to this point of public service. She has been steeled throughout her life in nerves, confidence and character and there is no doubt that Priscilla will always remain Priscilla regardless of external pressures. As she stood up to the playground bullies as a child, so she will stand up for those who are in the right. It is who she is. It is Priscilla.

While editing this book I myself have been inspired, not to be Priscilla but to be that strong leader that I desire to be in my small world. She has a vision not only for America, that it should retain its founding principles, but that women would be a significant part of it, not just in traditional roles but in high-profile positions, as world and national and city and family leaders. She sees that women have a valuable voice and that women bring more to the table when they function fully in their feminine strengths rather than by denying them. She wants to encourage the women out there to be undaunted in their desire for excellence.

Not to say she's not all for the men and boys too because she is fully supportive and respectful to the male compliment of female strengths. But as a woman who has forged her own way in a predominately male career-path, she wants to encourage all people to use their strengths for excellence, whatever they are. I believe she challenges us not to change or conform to the societal expectations of who we are or aren't. Priscilla has inspired me, and I hope she will you, too. She is this great and mighty thing and yet she is just a person too, and she is still, after all this time, my friend.

--Dominique Snedeker

Curiously Strong

## *Introduction*

It is quite humbling to expose my life's story in a book for the entire world to see. I hardly feel adequate to share my story as anything other than ordinary. Yet, as I meet young women all over the world, I can't help but want to applaud them for the inspiration they have provided me in becoming who I am. Many deserve to be acknowledged for their incredible strength during adversity. Conversely, I have also seen many who need to "woman-up" to the opportunities placed before them. The strength is there!

It is sobering when I pause to recognize the women in my lineage who have come before me and set the tone for stamina, endurance, and inner strength. I feel blessed to have been born into a family culture that expects women to perform at their best. It is my hope that my story will inspire young women to realize their own strength and to ultimately want to exceed the expectations of those around them.

As I have traveled around Idaho and spoken to various groups about female leadership, I have been encouraged to write down my biographical account. Many men and women have concerns about their daughters competing and succeeding in what they believe to be a man's world. I consider this to be a narrow view of reality. The proof of female strength is in the well-documented accomplishments of many women throughout history who have served as capable leaders. If my experience can help young women understand their God-given abilities, then I humbly lay it before them in this account and challenge each of them to learn from my experiences and exceed my performance. *"You Can Do It."*

Many of the stories I share in this book are quite personal. Some stories reference people who are still actively serving our country in the armed forces. For their protection, most of the names will be changed in my story.

It is not my intention in this account to dwell on the particular historical elements of a situation but instead to highlight how each of our *perceptions* is what truly matters, and how those interpretations and assessments can ultimately change the outcome of a person's life. In the end, each of our lives is a collection of events that culminate in feelings, thoughts and judgments that ultimately build the totality of our own experiences. What we feel, think and believe have more powerful impacts on our own growth and development than the external factors of the events or the pressures we get from other people.

I have selected stories and events that I think might be instructional to young people going through difficult times. I have purposefully chosen to share the situations where I was vulnerable and weak to demonstrate the strength that arises from the ashes of vulnerability and weakness when we are able to overcome them. I do not believe there is only one way to view these situations. I DO believe we are on this planet to grow and learn from many different circumstances.

# *Part One: Becoming Curiously Strong*

**be· com· ing** (1)

Verb

    1. to pass from one state to another.

**cu· ri· ous· ly**

Adverb

    1. having been made carefully.

**strong**

Adjective

    1. having the power to move heavy weights or perform other physically demanding tasks.

    2. physically powerful; having great muscular strength.

# Chapter 1

## A Legacy of Strong Women

As a little girl, I fondly remember seeing a popular poster of a strong woman with a flexed bicep and a determined look on her face. "Rosie the Riveter" was on television, on lunch boxes, and in art museums. She even found her way into my workout room. Looking back, I find it interesting that I had always admired Rosie for her strength and grit, but it wasn't until I was well into my thirties that I learned that my grandmother played a similar role as Rosie during World War II. This was an era when many strong women contributed in new ways to the fabric of America.

There was something unique about my grandmother's strength. Her family originated as sharecroppers in North Carolina and lived a simple but proud lifestyle. Eventually, they moved to Tennessee, Arkansas, and Oklahoma, where they experienced the dust bowl years. Even though they lived comparatively well as rural farmers through the Great Depression, my Grandma grew up not knowing what it meant to have nice things. However, there were things she did have, such as a strong work ethic, character, and resolve. It's funny how the importance of some of the invisible parts of life becomes apparent much later.

I am grateful to have come from a heritage of character and resolve that was passed on through day-to-day living. I also inherited many of her "family truisms." A few of my favorite sayings from Grandma include:

*"Soap is cheap."* There is no reason to be dirty.

*"Poor people have poor ways."* According to Grandma, this meant that having no money was different than being poor; she considered laziness true poverty. Because my Grandma always worked hard and had no respect for those who would not work, she never considered herself poor.

*"Use it up, wear it out, and make it do, or do without."* There is never a reason to be wasteful or make excuses based on "not having enough."

*"Don't let school get in the way of your education."* Learning opportunities and teachers are everywhere, not just in classrooms.

*"Three moves is as good as a fire."* All that stuff you've been saving is not as valuable as you think it is; if it isn't worth the effort of packing up and moving, it isn't worth keeping around. Packrat behavior and materialism was not an admirable trait in Grandma's family.

## Grandma's Grit

World War II challenged our nation's resolve so deeply that it asked our women to step into traditionally male roles to help with the war efforts. My grandmother was single and 24 years old when she answered the call to do her part. She took a job with Cactus Ordinance Works in Cactus, Texas and worked at the plant manufacturing ammonium nitrate, which was used in making war munitions. While there she met the man who would become my grandfather, a discharged Army sergeant who was her shop foreman. Soon after marrying, they moved to the Pacific Coast. There my grandmother took a job with Douglas Aircraft, where assembly lines operated by women were welding and riveting airplanes and ships.

By the time the War was over, my grandparents were well on their way to building a family. By 1951 they had five children–four sons and one daughter (my mother). Grandma stayed home with the children as was customary at the time, but they struggled on just one income. So, just after child number five was born in 1951, Grandma's strong will and dedicated work ethic drove her to change that situation. She decided to use education to improve her family's prospect. A few years later, my grandmother was the first and only person in her entire extended family to earn a college degree – plus a teaching credential to boot!

## *Strength and Grit in the Next Generation*

With Grandma's example of strength of character, it's not surprising that my mother developed a similar constitution. Her frugal parents didn't have money to spend on luxuries like new school clothes. That didn't bother their four boys too much, as they were able to share clothes and get by on less, but Mom didn't have that option. While ready-made clothes in the 1960s were expensive, fabric was very affordable, so around age 10 Mom learned to sew her own school clothes. Mom not only sewed her own clothes, but eventually designed them well enough to become the envy of her friends.

I believe she inherited her work ethic and strong-willed nature from her mother, but if you ask my mother, she'll say she acquired her grit by growing up with four brothers. Her formative years occurred in a house full of boys while her mom and dad were working, so she says it's in that environment where she learned to be competitive and strong.

If she could not catch the ball or hit homeruns, she was not included in the ball games. No whining. No tears. And if a ball hit you, you just sucked it up.

With that kind of toughness, it seemed natural for her to join a school sports team. At the time, few options existed for women in high school sports, so swimming was her choice. But she didn't just join the swim team. She went all in. My mother ended up breaking school records in the 100-meter freestyle, the backstroke, and as a member of the relay team.

Even with all these achievements, my mother remained quiet about it. Not out of humility, but because she thought that kind of effort was expected. In fact, I only recently learned that my mother broke all those records. I draw strength from knowing that my grandma's strong will and dedicated work ethic rubbed off on her children.

My mother also used those swimming skills to help her be self-sufficient by landing summer jobs as a lifeguard so she could pay her way through college. She witnessed the importance her own mother placed on education, so from her earliest years, going to college always felt like it was part of the plan. It wasn't discussed much, it was just expected.

Following her mother's example of hard work and determination, my mother graduated high school in three and a half years and went directly to college. She married young, juggled school, family, and work, and never slowed down. After earning her BA and getting a teaching credential, she continued to graduate school and earned two master's degrees. Eventually my mother became the principal of a K-12 school. That might not seem out of the ordinary today, but in the 1990s in Idaho, female high school principals were few and far between.

As well as progressing in her dynamic career, my strong professional working mother was already raising four other children before she had me. Although I don't remember it, six months after I was born we moved to a new house that was big enough to accommodate five kids. It wasn't just any big house though; it was custom-designed by my mom for the specific needs of our family. In fact, she and my dad did a lot of the construction work themselves so they could afford the bigger home.

This was my heritage; strong women demonstrating what a "can-do" mindset could accomplish.

# Curiously Strong

# Chapter 2

## Daddy's Girl

I've talked about the strong women in my lineage, but I learned strength and resilience from both parents. It was my father who taught me how to shoot, how to lift weights, to love God and our country, and that the strongest people aren't afraid of strength in others; instead they build on others' strengths. In fact, to say that I am a daddy's girl is quite an understatement.

My dad joined the Air Force long before I was born. He enlisted in 1965, at the height of the Vietnam War. He had grown up on a small family farm, and like me he was the youngest of five. His older brothers taught him how to shoot, and his BB gun was one of his favorite childhood treasures. When he outgrew the BB gun, he "graduated" to a .22-caliber rifle, and he practiced a lot. After enlisting, his keen understanding and respect for guns served him well in the military police.

My dad went to Vietnam and was part of a team that provided security for Phan Rang airbase, where F-4 fighter-bombers took off frequently. He would often patrol the end of the flight line at night, where he got to watch the jets take off. The volume and intensity of the jet engines made a huge impact on him, and he often shared those stories of awe with me as I was growing up. Although I never realized it at the time, his sincere love for America and his fond Air Force memories made deep impressions on me.

One day after his tour in Vietnam was over and he was stationed stateside, my dad was asked to try out for the Vandenberg Air Force Base shooting team. He made the team, and that started him down the road of competitive shooting. In short order, his childhood mastery of marksmanship earned him a trip to the 1967 annual Air Force World Wide match. He missed taking first place in combat shooting by only one shot.

My very first childhood memory was of my father. I couldn't have been more than two years old when he first introduced me to flying. Not the typical "let's go get in an airplane" kind of flying; it was more like short-term free-fall. With both of his hands firmly holding my sides, he would launch me into the air, and as I came rapidly hurtling back down toward the earth, I always felt as if I could really fly. Time after time he would give me little throws into the air, and I would always plead, "Do it again!" and, "Again!" Every time I floated through the air, free as a bird, looking down at the world, it felt like time stood still. Those moments made an imprint on my soul, and I went on to seek those birds-eye view perspectives throughout my life.

When I was five years old my dad helped me muscle up a shotgun to take my first shot. The target would go into the stew pot: a wild rabbit. I aimed and fired, but I missed. To my amazement, the rabbit didn't move. And so, Dad taught me how to quickly reload and shoot again. It wasn't until the third shot that I actually hit the target. To this day, I remember that I wasn't apprehensive about shooting the gun or bothered by how loud it was. I was just dumbfounded that the rabbit sat there and let me shoot at it three separate times.

I don't feel that there is any particular lesson to be learned from the rabbit not budging, but the steady, patient pragmatism I learned from my father helped me through many tough situations throughout my life. In addition to learning how to fire a weapon and the reality of shooting to kill, I also learned how to skin and clean that rabbit. Years later while I was in Air Force survival training, I was surreptitiously given the task of skinning a rabbit for my group's dinner. I made short work of it amidst all the "ooos" and "yucks" coming from my classmate. I was a country girl rock star that day. (If you've never had rabbit before, yes, it does taste like chicken.)

Curiously Strong

# Chapter 3

## The Pin-'em-Down Strategy

Growing up, I remember a very busy, fast-paced life. Expectations were high. Everyone helped. Both of my parents worked full time jobs, so I grew up with the understanding that all the chores had to be split up fairly. I heard it more than once: "If you are a part of this family, you have to help with the chores." In other words, I was accustomed to carrying my share of the load.

As soon as I was old enough I attended daycare and pre-kindergarten schooling so that my mom and dad could both work. I remember my first daycare provider whose name was Gloria. She had a cozy home with ruffled pink curtains that I loathed. As someone who was accustomed to being busy, I occasionally got into mischief, and to make matters worse I had two brothers at home who liked to egg me into daredevil situations. I pulled off many of the stunts that we came up with, but when I tried to show my daycare friends some of my new tricks, Mrs. Pink Curtains didn't think they were so cute.

One episode that has been repeated more than a few times over the years at family gatherings is the day I sat on Derek, another toddler in Gloria's care. Derek kept taking my toy, and I had grown quite frustrated with him. My solution was simple; there was no fussing, no crying, and it was no big deal. I simply knocked him over and sat squarely on his chest, retrieved my toy from his grip and happily continued playing with it. Derek flailed around and squirmed to get loose but remained firmly pinned to the floor. Whenever this story gets told, my mom usually reminds me that I haven't changed much.

Then there's the time I got in trouble for unrolling all the toilet paper in the bathroom. I still don't remember doing it, but I was found guilty. I was especially thankful when my parents finally arrived that day to rescue me from my uncomfortable predicament.

I don't consider myself a fighter, but when my sense of fair play kicks in, I have to say, it's like a switch gets flipped on. I prefer that everyone gets along, but I am not afraid of stepping up and taking charge to make sure things work out fairly.

Taking control of any unfair situation came rather easy for me as a kid because I was big for my age. I grew quickly, just like both of my grandmothers did, and by age 10 I was 5'9" and 160 pounds. My father was 6'4" and his two brothers were taller than him, so I had secretly hoped that I would be as tall as my aunts who were over six feet. When I stopped growing at the age of 10, I must admit I was sorely disappointed.

Still, being the biggest girl on the playground at school had its advantages, because so many kids thought I was a teacher! My fellow elementary schoolmates would come up to me on the playground crying if they fell down. They would run to me shouting that Johnny stole their dodge ball, or they would ask me if it was okay to go to the bathroom. Granted, as a fellow student, my actual authority was very limited, but there were several instances where I found ways to administer playground justice—and I liked it. I liked being an advocate for fairness.

Being the playground "teacher" was amusing, but being the biggest girl on the playground was rather lonely at times. I remember a thin girl who temporarily called herself my friend. She came up to me specifically to ask me about my weight. She told me that she had been talking about me to her mother, and her mother had explained that I couldn't help how big I was, and that I wasn't actually fat, I was just "big-boned." I did not enjoy being called big-boned. It wasn't like I could control the size of my bones, but it didn't matter. It felt like I wasn't quite good enough to be her friend, simply because of the size of my bones.

Having big bones also meant I didn't get to sit with the trendy, rich girls at lunch, because I didn't look like them. My size wasn't the only difference there. They all brought their lunches to school, packed by their mothers, and I had to go through the cafeteria line. Being a girl in the American school system can be overwhelming. There are so many expectations, and kids can be so cruel. It brings tears to my eyes just thinking about the pressure of junior high school, being too small, or too big, or too anything. There are some things in life that can't be pinned down physically. It takes time to learn how to deal with them.

Curiously Strong

## Chapter 4

## *A New Appreciation for Freedom*

About the time I turned 10, my older siblings were out of the house and on their own, and my mother was offered a year-long sabbatical job opportunity. The position was as the high school guidance counselor at an American International School in Kfar Shmaryahu, Israel. I remember Mom's phone call home before she accepted the job. She wanted to confirm with Dad and me that this yearlong overseas job would be okay with us as a family. I was excited about the adventure, and the timing was good; my dad's job allowed him to "commute" to Israel and live with us every other month during the school year. It was during this mother-daughter adventure halfway around the world that my eyes were opened to cultures and events bigger than any I had ever imagined.

## *Eyes Wide Open*

In America, it's during the Thanksgiving holiday that many children are taught the need to be grateful for what they have, and it's during our July 4th Independence Day celebrations that children are taught the concept of patriotism. I thought I had learned those things growing up, but when I moved to Israel the concepts of gratitude and patriotism were pressed much more deeply into my heart. At first, life in Israel was peaceful and beautiful; it didn't seem much different from my life in the United States. During our first few weeks we settled in and toured historic sites on the weekends. After about a month, reality started to surface.

It was the mid-1990s, and Israel was in a state of sporadic war, with potential terrorist attacks lurking around every corner. I vividly remember the day that reality confronted me. My mother and I were walking home from the grocery store to our flat (the Israeli term for an apartment) when we saw an entire street corner being cordoned off because of a bomb scare.

As neither of us had ever witnessed anything like that before, my mom and I lingered in the distance to watch what was happening. The streets were filled with sirens as law enforcement officials quickly put up barricades to keep people away. Even in all the commotion (of what seemed to me like a monumental event), the people on the street acted as if it were quite ordinary. We soon learned that they were accustomed to these safety precautions.

We also learned that law enforcement officials selected an area to cordon off based on the size of the package that contained the suspected bomb. That day, the package was relatively small—a grocery bag sitting underneath a bus stop bench. Within minutes, an armored truck pulled up and the bomb squad quickly deployed a bomb-detecting robot. I watched in awe; I had never seen anything like that before. After a short time, the bomb squad team announced that the robot had determined the bag was not a threat. It was simply a frozen chicken that someone had accidently left behind. A frozen chicken?! Seriously?

The Israeli people had grown accustomed to all these safety precautions, but the inconvenience was entirely justified on the rare occasions that bombs actually went off. When they did, people had also grown accustomed to dealing with the fallout. Interestingly, I also found out that most family homes in Israel had what's known as a safe room—a concrete bunker—for when they were threatened with more serious military attacks. I was constantly amazed at the way the entire country of Israel lives in a state of caution and preparedness.

When I was living in Israel, the country was well prepared for bomb detection with technology that was ahead of its time. They also had quick-reaction motorcycle volunteers that could respond with first aid to any situation in a matter of minutes. It was like the entire country was trained and prepared to live in the middle of what seemed like a war zone while at the same time going about their daily lives in a clean, beautiful environment.

> **"Freedom" suddenly had much deeper meaning–a meaning that I felt.**

My time in Israel taught me to be grateful for the safety and security of living in America. We didn't have bomb threats in America when I was growing up. In fact, it was something I had never even thought about before. But those experiences in Israel also taught me about patriotism and the value of freedom. Freedom was no longer just a buzzword that we used on the holidays. After experiencing the ever-present threat of war all around me, the word "Freedom" suddenly had much deeper meaning–a meaning that I felt.

Being near ground zero for a bomb threat instantly awakened my senses to the presence of fear and showed me that fear is the antithesis of freedom. In America I had never experienced real fear, the kind of fear where your life is in jeopardy because somebody doesn't like you or your way of life.

Also, in America I wasn't exposed to the horrors of terrorism. My overseas experience in Israel taught me to cherish America and made me aware that there were good reasons to be proud to be Americans. I realized that living without fear (that is, living in freedom) was something worth fighting for so that more people in the world could experience it.

Despite occasional chaos in the streets, I found it interesting that the crime rate in Israel was very, very low. In reflection, I think it had something to do with the fact that almost every other person carried a rifle in full view. At the age of 18 everyone serves in the armed forces (three years for men, two years for women) so they are constantly coming and going between home and their military duty stations (carrying their weapons with them). The other factor, I believe, was the unity they felt as people because the vast majority had moved to Israel by choice. They felt strong as a people and culture.

While I attended the private international school where my mother was a counselor, I was humbled by my classmates. Many were children of foreign diplomats or other high-profile people, and all were world travelers. Yet, they were all very down-to-earth, regular kids. My best friend, Sonya, was the daughter of a diamond mine owner from South Africa. I also fondly remember a kindergarten girl from South Africa who was fluent in four languages—she actually helped the teachers translate! I was impressed by her skills. I was "asked out" (fifth grade definition) for the first time by a professional basketball player's son. Another good friend was originally from India; born to parents that did not want a girl and adopted by an American Embassy diplomat.

I took required classes in Hebrew and found it entertaining that I learned the language faster than my mother. I felt quite proud; this may have been the first time I felt I could do something better than Mom.

After school each afternoon, I would wait for my mother to finish her work as a guidance counselor. I usually did my homework while sitting at a table across the room from her small meetings. Every day from three o'clock until five, she provided guidance to seniors and their parents about college entrance. Most of the students, even those from other countries, wanted to attend college in America; my mom would guide them through the application process. While sitting across the room, I got to listen.

During one of her college admissions appointments, I overheard her talking about United States military academies. She talked about West Point, Annapolis, and the Air Force Academy as prestigious four-year colleges where students earn a commission as officers and leaders in the military, where, ultimately, they fight for the freedoms and other American values. My ears perked up. Knowing that my mother and father had both paid their own way through college, I figured that I was likely going to have to do the same thing. When I found out that attending college at one of the academies was paid for by the military, I set my first long-term goal. I was only 10 years old, but I set a goal to get accepted into the United States Air Force Academy in Colorado Springs.

I had lots of questions for Mom on the way home that day. All of her answers seemed just right for me, so I decided that starting that day, I would do better in school so I could meet the standard expected by the Academy. Mom's summarizing comment was so typical of her, "If you really want to, you can do it." There was no doubt in her voice, nor any skeptical side-look. She believed in me and proceeded to set out the clear expectations of what I would have to do to achieve my goal. In keeping with my family heritage, I set to work so I could get it done.

It was a great year for meeting interesting and diverse people. The experiences opened my eyes to new and exciting horizons and broadened my view of how the world worked outside of America.

## *Chapter 5*

## *Breaking Sweat*

After we moved back to the States, something else happened that influenced the direction of my life. My dad knew I didn't like being called "big-boned." He was big-boned as well. So, after assessing my situation and my athletic potential, one day he said, "Honey, it doesn't look like you're going to be a ballerina. Let's hit the gym!"

Now, the gym seemed like a peculiar place for a teenage girl to go. This was Idaho in the nineties, and gyms were not the trendy, popular places they were in the major cities. I imagined them mostly to be small, dark, stinky places where old men hung out.

When I was younger, I remembered my dad talking about "hitting the gym" with his work buddies, where they would do things like bench press and curls. I remember hearing him talk about those lifts. That didn't seem like something girls did, especially girls who were about to turn 13. Most of the girls my age were into dance lessons or gymnastics. These were things I never took interest in, mainly because I couldn't relate to them; you know, "big bones" and all. Therefore, I was open, albeit a bit skeptical, when Dad suggested that he and I "hit the gym" together.

At the time, I had just entered the 7th grade, and we were living near a small rural town called Ririe, Idaho, northeast of Idaho Falls. Ririe was a farm town with a bustling population just over five hundred, close to the Snake River at the base of the Teton Mountains. Just up the road was the Palisades

Dam, where we would fish between swats at the endless mosquitoes. We spent our winters skiing at the Kelly Canyon ski area and our summers at the Heise Hot Springs. But my absolute favorite thing to do was driving over to Swan Valley to get a scoop of square ice cream. Yes, square ice cream. Travelers from all over the world would stop at that small roadside store to get a scoop of that special square-shaped treat.

The middle school I attended didn't have a weight lifting room, but Dad worked it out so that he and I were able to use the high school gym in the evening or early morning. Since we used the gym only during those hours, I was never worried about anyone else being there—we always had the place to ourselves.

I was just 13 when Dad started teaching me the basics of lifting. Looking back, learning how to lift weights was the beginning of many valuable lessons in my personal growth. Powerlifting was in many ways a metaphor for the challenges that I would face in the coming years, and as I reflect now, was a major factor in developing strength, determination, endurance, and accomplishment. Who could have guessed that pumping iron would be so useful to a young girl for the next 15 years and beyond?

On that first day in the gym, we jumped right into bench-pressing. Dad started by having me lift the bar without any weights on it. I remember it wobbling back and forth the first time. Then he would work in a few sets for himself, but he kept it light by throwing on some 45-pound plates on each side in between my sets. I say he "kept it light," but those 45-pound plates were huge to me. Then, together we would go through the routine of pulling off his 45-pound plates so that I could do a set with just the bar. I felt pretty pathetic lifting only the bar, so I quickly set a goal to increase the amount I could lift.

Of all the different kinds of weight lifts I've done, bench-pressing remains my favorite. It is the lift that defines you as a weight lifter. Even though it seems like a simple, short exercise, there is a lot of technique involved. You can assess a lot about a lifter based on how they bench press. For instance, some lifters are lazy and don't lock out their elbows at the top. Others try to cheat and bounce the bar off their chest in an effort to defeat gravity at the bottom. But a good, clean bench press is the ultimate display of brute upper body strength.

It took only a couple of weeks before I had 25-pound plates on each side. I learned that the first part to increasing the amount of weight you lift was to mentally accept the challenge. Then you had to load the bar and try to lift the new weight off the rack.

Timing was the next thing to consider, because if you lower the bar too quickly, the weight will sink into your chest and you won't be able to counter it and push it back up. If you lower it too slowly, you will tire out your muscles and they will reach fatigue with the bar sitting on your chest. The perfect bench press is one in which you lower the bar slowly and steadily in one fluid motion, and then just tap it to your chest as you reverse the direction.

After a while I could do 10 repetitions with the flow coming together like the rhythm of a song. Many times, while putting the weight back into the rack after a good set, my dad would say "nice job." Those words always brought a smile to my face.

Just a few short months after we started, we no longer needed to take the 45-pound plates off in between sets. I was lifting as much as my dad! I knew he could lift much more, but it was like he set goals for me without me knowing it. Bench-pressing 150 pounds became the next milestone for me, and I was gaining confidence.

One day we were lifting early in the morning and some of the high school's football players walked in on our routine. Normally I would have been embarrassed, but with my dad there spotting me as I did multiple repetitions with the "big plates" on the bar, I was beaming on the inside. Those football players were watching me do my reps with 135 pounds on the bar, and they could tell I was strong.

## *Chapter Six*

## *A Strong Mentor*

My parents saw how much I enjoyed doing the workouts, so they bought a family membership to the YMCA in Idaho Falls. At first it felt a little strange going to a large gym with lots of people around, but my dad taught me to walk into the gym confidently. He reminded me that I had just as much of a right to the equipment as any other person there. That was fine, but there were so many more machines to use! Among them were setups for inclines, declines, and military presses, so we started doing them all, and, there is where I met Linda Higgins.

Linda was one of the few women in the gym. She was also a personal trainer. Prior to becoming a trainer, she was a bodybuilder and world champion powerlifter, even though she weighed barely a hundred pounds herself. Linda watched me bench-pressing one day. Much to my surprise, she invited me to compete in a bench press competition that she and her husband, Mike, were hosting at the Idaho Falls YMCA. I had never bench pressed on a stage in front of an audience before, but hesitantly, I agreed. Not long after that, Linda agreed to be my weightlifting coach and train me for competitions. With her encouragement, I became a regular gym attendee all throughout my high school years. In fact, sometimes I would go to the "Y" four or five times a week!

After becoming my coach, Linda introduced me to a new lift that rivaled the bench press as my favorite: the squat. I must admit, the real reason I liked it so much was because I could usually outshine the boys by squatting more weight than they could.

Going to the gym more regularly I started to notice the gym habits of other people. I noticed that most guys spent their gym time doing upper body exercises. It made sense, because that is where they are naturally stronger, and it's also where they see the quickest results. On the other hand, women tend to be naturally strong in their lower body, and sure enough, I noticed many women working on their legs and glutes.

This insight helped me realize why I enjoyed squatting. My bench press gains only happened a few pounds at a time. But during a squat workout, I could easily add twenty pounds on a good day. Still, it was Linda's constant encouragement that motivated me to improve. She would say things like, "You were born to squat!" That might sound kind of weird, but it was a huge inspiration to reach down inside myself and give more than I thought I could.

Developing my squatting abilities also helped me with my other sporting events. After I was in high school I joined the track team, where I started throwing the shot put and discus. Interestingly, it seemed like the more weight I could squat, the further I could put the shot. It intrigued me that developing my strengths in one area also created positive impacts in other areas.

## My 400 lb. Life

It was also while I was in high school that Linda got me involved in powerlifting competitions. I already did bench presses and squats, but the third lift in a powerlifting competition is the deadlift. Although the deadlift was made popular in the mid-eighteenth century, I humorously imagine that it started in ancient Rome with a bunch of bored men deciding to test their manhood by picking up heavy objects. But, because I wanted to do powerlifting competitions, I learned to do the deadlift. It certainly wasn't my favorite. The only reason I liked it was because I could lift 400 pounds off the floor. It became a personal challenge. It wasn't easy, but I could do it!

Some of the exercises Linda taught me that greatly improved my deadlift capability were strength drills called "negatives." Negatives were sets that you did at the end of a workout that were so ridiculously heavy that you couldn't complete the lift even if you wanted—you would just bear the weight as you restrained it against gravity. For negatives, we would put 400 pounds on the squat rack; I would step up under it, lift it off, and lower it to the bottom position. From there, the spotters would take the weight so that I didn't have to stand back up with it—which would have been impossible, anyway.

Negatives were rather painful, but they made me feel great afterwards, plus they helped me make huge strength gains. The psychology behind them is the key to their success. If all you ever do is challenge your muscles with weight they already can lift, you can only make slow, gradual improvements (as it is with most things). However, if you burden your muscles with more than they are used to—that is, tell them you expect more from them after they're already drained—then they try to compensate the next time around. You get stronger, faster by

> **You get stronger, faster by challenging yourself with things outside your ability.**

challenging yourself with things outside your ability—life lesson to remember.

With Linda's encouragement, I signed up for full powerlifting competitions, which consist of three maximum lifts in the squat, bench press, and deadlift. My successes at these regional events qualified me to compete at the World Powerlifting Congress national competition, so off we all went to Fresno, California. At that event I broke the national records for my age and weight class and qualified for the world meet.

Amazingly, as a teenager, I set world records for my age and weight class in all three lifts: the squat, the bench press, and the deadlift. Linda continued to train me over the next few years, and I continued to break world records along the way.

## Sun Valley X-Press

So what else can one do with this weightlifting ability? Well, later in high school, I attended a leadership conference for teens in Sun Valley, Idaho. Toward the end of the course, the instructors said that one of the requirements was to perform some kind of talent on stage, in front of all the other attendees. I was mortified. I didn't have any talents, and I certainly wasn't going to fake my way through a ballet piece! Thankfully, a friend from my old neighborhood who knew I was a weight lifter came up with an idea: I could do a human bench press. It was genius! We ironed out the details, and our plan worked beautifully. He and I took the stage, and two spotters lifted his toothpick-shaped, 140-pound body up onto my arms. From there, I bench pressed him—multiple times. The crowd loved it!

> **Good leaders identify the talents of others and use them for everyone's gain.**

The cool thing is that he too went on to graduate from the Air Force Academy and is now an F-16 pilot. I doubt he shares the story of being bench pressed by a girl (or worse, an A-10 pilot!), but he taught me a neat lesson about leaders: good leaders identify the talents of others and use them for everyone's gain.

## Building Strength

Building strength has been my key to overcoming fear and increasing my confidence. Along the way I have become more able to take on greater challenges and face trials and adversity with boldness. Strength begins with modest baby steps, grows with small challenges, and then provides the boldness to step forward as opportunities arrive.

I really liked being strong, and the training taught me vital lessons about self-discipline, goal setting, and how to push myself to the limits—both mentally and physically. I learned that if I set my mind to it, I can do more than I think I can. Weight lifting also gave me self-assurance and a kind of courage I didn't know I had. I will forever be grateful for Dad, Mike, and Linda, who saw my potential and equipped me with the personal development skills so vital to my future success.

Curiously Strong

## *Chapter 7*

## *The Salmon River Experience*

At the beginning of my junior year, my mother finished another advanced degree and was offered a job as the principal of a K-12 school in Riggins, Idaho. After another family talk, she accepted. This meant another move. Not to a different country, just to the other side of the state.

Riggins sits right at the confluence of the main Salmon River and the Little Salmon River, the area of Idaho that is often referred to as the whitewater capital of the world. As such, the town of 500 is a tourist destination, and tourism is the primary source of revenue for its incredible fishing, hunting, rafting and hiking. Riggins also sits right below Seven Devils National Park—seven jagged peaks that jut straight up between the two deepest canyons in the United States, Hells Canyon and the Salmon River Canyon. Even though it was challenging to move during my high school years, I grew especially fond of Riggins because the people were authentic, and the women were strong.

It was good for me to witness my mother transition into her new job. She took on the position as one of the only female high school principals in the state at that time. It wasn't until years later that I fully understood the impact of this career choice for her. Through watching her, I witnessed what it was like for a smart, talented woman to step into what had long been considered a man's world and succeed. I admired her straightforward focus and her grit.

My longstanding goal was to get accepted into the Air Force Academy, so I stayed in overdrive my junior and senior years. I needed to show them I was serious. After all, the application process and resume requirements for acceptance into a military academy are more demanding than typical colleges. Military academies look for students who excel in five distinct pillars of development: academic, athletic, leadership, community service, and spiritual development, and I wanted every aspect covered.

Keep in mind that during my high school years, the Internet was not what it is today. Back then, the Academy had "pre-candidate cards" you could send in, and they would send you a booklet outlining what it typically took to get accepted. I requested one every year. In those booklets they would list what kind of grades and SAT scores they were looking for, as well as other things from those five pillars to round out your resume.

During those two years of high school in Riggins, I continued my weight lifting, I kept very busy with my studies, and I also joined the volleyball, basketball and track teams. It was an extremely full schedule, but it all worked out because I didn't have much of a social calendar. When your mother is the school principal and your father the local deputy sheriff, it's not like too many kids are interested in inviting you to their social events.

The Academy's booklet also said that the average cadet has student body leadership experience, so I ran for and was elected to represent my junior class. During my senior year I ran for student body president, and I won by just one vote! That was when it struck me that every person's vote really does matter, and that it is important to vote for yourself, too!

Every service academy hopeful must receive a congressional nomination even to be considered for admission to the Air Force Academy. I was fortunate to receive three nominations. My congressional representative wrote a letter nominating me, as did both of my state's US senators.

Remaining diligent in school, I studied hard, and received straight A's. At the end of my senior year, this earned me the honor of being class valedictorian.

My heart was set on getting accepted to the Air Force Academy, so I spent all four years of high school in overdrive and put into action what my mother had told me all those years ago in Israel: "If you really want to, you can do it."

## Acceptance into the Academy

My high school basketball coach (who did double duty as one of my teachers) and all my fellow players had known it was my goal to attend the Air Force Academy but were perplexed that I didn't have a backup plan. They wondered what I would do if I wasn't accepted, and most thought I should also apply to Boise State University or the University of Idaho as a backup plan. I didn't mention I had been offered and turned down a scholarship to the University of Idaho; I wanted to serve my country and staying local was not an option. If I couldn't get accepted at the Air Force Academy, my backup plan was West Point or Annapolis.

Early during my senior year, my goal became a little more real when the Air Force Academy sent its track coach to my high school to visit with me. He was checking to see how serious I was, and probably to decide whether they wanted to recruit me onto their track team at the Academy. After that visit I didn't hear anything, so I just kept up with my overdrive schedule.

One day in January, I came home from school and my dad handed me a letter. It was from the Air Force Academy. Upon opening it, I learned that the Academy wanted me, and they also wanted me on their track team. It stated as long as I kept my grades up for the rest of the school year, I was in!

After all the effort and focus that I had spent on achieving my goal, one might expect that the best day of my senior year would have been when I received that letter informing me that I had been officially selected to attend the Air Force Academy. I had been so utterly focused on getting in that receiving the actual letter was almost anticlimactic.

The next morning, we had an early basketball practice. I told the team about the letter, and everyone was excited for me. A few days later we were playing a tournament at the University of Idaho, and while we were there, my coach and some friends from my basketball team took me to a hair salon to cut off my long hair. At the time, it was a requirement for new female cadets to have short hair, and they wanted to get me ready!

## *Chapter 8*

## *Bring Me Men*

Arriving at the campus of the United States Air Force Academy puts awe in every new cadet's heart. The Base chapel has seventeen spires and serves as a visual centerpiece of the campus with the majestic Rocky Mountains as a backdrop. The student-manned Air Force planes flying overhead infuse cadets with motivation, and the mile-high elevation of Colorado Springs literally takes your breath away—from lack of oxygen. The Academy is a magnificent place, but the day a new cadet shows up, the only thing on her mind is not throwing up from nervousness.

> **Good leaders must first know how to follow.**

Freshmen at the Academy are technically known as Four-Degree cadets, but mostly they are called "Doolies." It's a word derived from the Greek word *doulos*, which means servant. The primary role for all Doolies is to learn how to be a good follower, because good leaders must first know how to follow. As cadets get promoted from Doolies to "Three-Degrees," "Two-Degrees" and then "Firsties" (seniors), they are also continually promoted into new leadership positions. Interestingly, some of my most valuable lessons on leadership were learned from experiencing bad leadership from my peers.

During our in-processing day in the early summer of 2001, all the new Doolies were taken by bus to the new cadet area. Emblazoned on the base of the ramp leading up to the cadet area were the words "Bring Me Men." I personally liked the phrase, and it never occurred to me that it might be construed to be sexist. Later this motto became controversial and was removed during the fallout from a campus sexual assault scandal.

## An Instant Shift of Focus

Nearly everyone remembers what he or she was doing on September 11, 2001. I distinctly remember sitting in a freshman chemistry class at the Air Force Academy when the news hit that airplanes had struck the Twin Towers in New York. From my classroom seat I looked out the window at the huge mountain topped with antenna towers that served the North American Aerospace Defense (NORAD). The entire Air Force Academy went on a lock down as the nation braced for any further attacks.

The events of September 11th, 2001 definitively changed my perspective on my future Air Force career. The same terrorism that I saw affecting Israel as a child was now in my own backyard. This could not be allowed to persist. The liberties and freedoms that defined our country were now under attack. I wanted to fight back, and this resolve reached down to my core. I wanted to give everything I had to stand for freedom and justice. Although I had not given much consideration to the idea previously, after that day the possibility of flying fighter planes was certainly on the table.

## Words Have Impact

In the spring of 2003, when I was finishing my Three-Degree (sophomore) year, the newspapers were highlighting the Air Force Academy, but not in a good way. According to reports, an unusually large number of sexual assaults had occurred at the Academy over the previous decade. In fact, just in the two years prior, 100 reports had been filed—resulting in zero convictions.

In Washington, D.C., this news shocked Capitol Hill into action. They initiated military inquiries at all three service academies. Needless to say, my life as a female cadet changed instantly. All the female cadets were asked to take surveys about our experiences, and in an attempt to provide safety through geographical segregation, we were required to move our belongings to new rooms—rooms that were next to the female bathrooms.

Campus life changed from that point forward. Most notably, the men started treating us differently. They were more hesitant to talk with us or to invite a female to one of their study groups. We went from being their fellow Airmen, to a liability that they needed to steer clear from.

As the scandal lingered over the ensuing months, we saw multiple changes implemented on campus. For example, as Colonels and Generals discussed ways to stop a culture that condoned negative treatment towards women, the "Bring Me Men" ramp ended up being changed. After all, words have meaning, and when those words are displayed prominently, they have significant impact on the organizational climate.

The words, "Bring Me Men," were replaced with the Air Force's core values:

*Integrity first, Service before self, Excellence in all we do.*

That marked a culture shift for the Academy and the Air Force in general. It was the first step in showcasing to the world that men and women working together in the military are stronger. In the area of women in leadership and combat there is still much to be learned, but cultural changes come slowly.

Even though the Academy's leadership had inherited rather than created the problem, the Academy Superintendent, Lt. General Dallager, was demoted to Major General, and retired soon after. Three other top leaders were also replaced.

It was a difficult time to be at the Academy for both men and women, but I remember being inspired with news that Colonel Debra Gray would be the new Vice-Commandant. Colonel Gray was the epitome of grace under fire. She was one of the 157 women who graduated from the Air Force Academy in 1980, the first class that included women.

As soon as Colonel Gray stepped into her new leadership position, she started meeting with female cadets in small groups to get our perspectives and ideas on how to improve the situation on campus. We appreciated her communication, encouragement, and the solid example of good leadership she made by making contact with her subordinates.

Several subtle but important things started changing. It was slow and sometimes uncomfortable. Mandatory training on gender bias and work place discrimination helped to define and clarify exactly what behaviors were problematic. In this atmosphere both male and female behaviors were under scrutiny. Overall, I think it was a healthy evaluation of how cultural norms and gender prejudices can and should be questioned. Those who chose to cling to an erroneous attitude and mindset toward the opposite sex were put on notice that they would be dealt with appropriately. This adjustment was necessary and good for the strength of the organization.

## Soaring

I had never piloted a plane prior to arriving at the Air Force Academy. That changed during the summer before my Three-Degree (sophomore) year when I had the opportunity to fly in the Academy's soaring program, the largest glider operation in the world. I participated with one of many small groups of other cadets which spent three weeks learning how to soar in a glider—an engineless aircraft with exceptionally long wings to give it more lift.

Each morning I would climb into a small glider with an instructor who was a more senior cadet. The glider would be hooked up by cable to a small engine-powered tow aircraft that would drag the glider behind it. Once we had been pulled up into the sky, the tow plane would release our tow strap and we would be free to fly along and enjoy the grand view of the mountains of Colorado's Front Range.

If there were ever a way to describe the feeling of freedom, it would be soaring. It is an astonishing feeling to be slowly succumbing to the pull of gravity, and then be pushed back upward by wind currents. It's as if you're floating in a delicate tug-of-war between air molecules. This weightless feeling of independence and freedom is both refreshing and invigorating, and completely quiet.

With the control stick in your hand, you establish the direction for which way you want to go, but you must manage the balance between updrafts and gravity to stay airborne. Some of the student instructors who master the knowledge of wind currents and powerless flight have stayed in the air for up to six hours and traveled as far as 200 miles from the base runway.

Learning to fly that summer was inspirational. After enduring the grind of my freshman year and the shock of the 9/11 attacks, flying free above Colorado's Front Range while looking down at the Academy helped strengthen my focus for why I was there: freedom and justice.

## *Chapter 9*

## *Beyond the Books*

Prior to being officially accepted, the Academy track team had expressed interest in my throwing ability. When I was accepted into the Academy I joined the team, where I threw the discus, the shot put, and the hammer. In Track and Field sports, the hammer is not a carpenter's tool; it's a heavy metal ball like a shot put that's connected to a grip by a strong steel wire.

Because I was a thrower, a large part of my workout regimen required intense weightlifting, which didn't bother me in the slightest. After all those years of weightlifting in high school I felt quite confident in the Academy's gym— even around the more senior cadets. I got involved in the powerlifting club and eventually became the club's president.

The members of my team were my friends, and we enjoyed participating in the tri-service powerlifting competitions with the Army's West Point cadets and the Navy's Annapolis midshipmen. In time, I shared stories about my world-record victories; before I knew it, my history as a weight lifter traveled throughout my squadron. Word travels quickly in the Air Force. In fact, my reputation as being a strong weight lifter even preceded me to pilot training after the Academy.

In an organization that was predominately comprised of men, weightlifting provided me with an equalizing factor; not because it made me competitive in a man's world, but because it was something men admired and at times envied. After a while, I sort of enjoyed having the male eyes in the room watching me squat 400 pounds.

Although I enjoyed the lifting competitions, throwing the hammer became my new love. I no longer squatted to achieve maximums; I squatted to become a better hammer thrower. My fellow throwers became my best friends and we worked together day-in and day-out. We'd eat together, throw together, lift together, eat some more and throw some more. We had contests among ourselves to see who could throw the farthest, who could eat the most, and who could put on the most lean-weight.

Unfortunately for some of their athletes, the Air Force maintains strict weight standards, which was fine while competing with the other military academies but proved to be a huge limiting factor for our NCAA Division I throwing team. As a child, I never dreamed I would one day be considered small. But our competitors were college students from places like Colorado State University, Berkley, and Brigham Young University, where their throwers did not have weight restrictions. Our relatively skinny athletes were beaten every year by the top female throwers in our conference. One girl was so large from food and weights that her trapezoid muscles sort of went from her chin to her shoulders; we gave her the endearing name of "No Neck." I can only imagine what her calorie consumption must have been.

As we needed so many calories, we throwers tended to view our entire track team's caloric intake as a group effort. The throwing team often sat next to the track team's long-distance runners at lunch and cheerfully ate their untouched meals, especially their desserts. We also spent hours running long distances after our weights and sprints to stay below our weight standards. We juggled the size issue constantly, too small for Division I and too large for the Air Force.

Despite all our challenges, we all felt on top of the world, and I thrived in an environment where there were other strong women who were equally motivated to use their God-given talents. We were living out the Air Force's core value of "excellence in all we do" on our way to becoming officers and leaders.

## *Too Nice?*

At the Academy there were a few friends who challenged me, and they taught me a thing or two along the way. My first serious boyfriend, Don, was one of those people. Don was an athlete, so he spent as much time at the gym as I did. Almost every day after dinner he would stop by my room to update me on the events of his day. Every night, no matter how much homework I had, I would listen to his stories. He shared his goals, ambitions, and future plans. He was going to become a fighter pilot.

After hearing Don talk about his fighter pilot dreams repeatedly, one day I mentioned that I too would find it cool to be a fighter pilot. Don's surprising response lingers with me to this day. He said, "You're too nice to be a fighter pilot." At the time, it seemed like a typical guy comment, but I've come to realize that those words have many implications— including the idea that to win, one must dispense with being nice and instead exhibit power.

Over the years, I have heard those words numerous times, and they still confuse me; "You're too nice to be a fighter pilot." What? Nice people don't defend America? I strongly believe that a woman can be kind, nice, live an honorable life, and still be a warrior who defends what she believes in. The words "mother bear" come to mind.

## A New Perspective of Israel

The summer after my Two-Degree (junior) year, I participated in a military trip overseas. During that trip, it was reinforced within me that not all cultures share the same values. In fact, some cultures have distorted the definitions of honor, freedom, and justice into something unrecognizable —murder, enslavement and deceit.

> I strongly believe that a woman can be kind, nice, live an honorable life, and still be a warrior who defends what she believes in.

I applied for a summer study program through the Academy with the Jewish Institute for National Security of America (JINSA). This is a pro-Israel nonprofit think tank that works on intergovernmental relations to help with issues of national security. I was particularly curious to learn about the Israeli Defense Force and how it compared to the civilian life in Israel that I had known as a child. I was grateful to be selected, along with 15 other cadets from the Air Force Academy, West Point, and Annapolis. JINSA conducts these study programs for military and civilian national security decision-makers to promote both American and Israeli interests.

Our group spent three weeks traveling throughout Israel learning about the country's military capabilities. I was impressed to see their F-16 aircraft, and most surprised to meet their fighter pilots. Their pilots were much younger than our pilots. It turns out that in Israel, students start their flight training while still in their version of the Air Force Academy, not afterwards as the United States does.

On one of our stops to an Israeli Defense Force base, we were introduced to a man named Daniel. He was a very large man who had been recruited into Israeli special operations. He was easily over 6'5" and a fit 225 pounds; men this large are not very common in Israel.

Dan had an incredible story of triumph and determination, and he shared his story with us—his "ground zero experience" with terrorism.

Dan told us about being on a security detail one summer evening in 2002, near a hotel in downtown Jerusalem. Dan observed a suspicious man wearing a bulky jacket enter the hotel lobby, so he followed behind the suspect. The man walked past the front desk and into a lobby full of couches and overstuffed chairs next to the hotel's elevators. Dan walked up to the man and confronted him. The man turned, and with a death stare in his eyes pulled out a hand-held trigger device. Dan recognized what was about to happen and tried to jump toward a nearby couch; milliseconds later, he was in the air as the deranged suicide bomber's explosion ripped through the hotel lobby.

Dan spent months in the hospital and underwent countless surgeries. Doctors said the only reason he survived was because he was about fifty pounds overweight at the time and the visceral fat in his torso shielded his vital organs. My heart filled with immense compassion as I sat across the table from him while he recounted this story; he had literally stood toe-to-toe with evil, looking into the eyes of terrorism at ground zero. Fortunately, Dan lived to tell this tale and turned his tragedy into action, becoming a leading expert and spokesman on counter-terrorism.

After recounting his story, Dan laughed and told us that his mother hadn't wanted him to go on an upcoming trip to America, where he would be teaching at a counter-terrorism conference. When we asked him why she didn't want him to go, he responded that she was worried that he would be shot. Ironically it was statistically more dangerous to be on the streets in America than in Israel. An interesting statistic to say the least; Dan laughed, but I had difficulty finding the humor. It actually made me sad.

## *A Lesson on Honor*

During our studies in Israel we also had the humbling opportunity of meeting some Holocaust survivors. I remembered one older gentleman who had shared with us how he had been imprisoned in a concentration camp, and how the prisoners were stripped of all their dignity. If you've read anything about the humiliation and degradation that people endured in those camps, you get the picture. He told us how the people he was with would get together regularly and pray.

He told us that one day they were outside doing their daily chores when they looked up to see huge formations of American bomber planes flying overhead. He said they stopped what they were doing, gathered together and prayed with all their might that the Americans would bomb them in their camp so that they could die with dignity and honor.

That story had a mind-blowing impact on me. These people had been stripped of everything, and all they wanted was to die with honor. In the end, the principle that remained dearest to their souls, the thing that they held to most tightly was their human honor—their individual self-respect.

Freedom. Liberty. Dignity and Honor. These are the principles that form the bedrock of America and the United States Constitution. I have always felt blessed to have grown up in a country where these concepts are written into our founding documents and are intended to be a part of our cultural fabric. The individual has worth and innate rights regardless of group identity.

Curiously Strong

## *Chapter 10*

## *Leadership Laboratory*

The mission of the Air Force Academy is "to educate, train, and inspire men and women to become leaders of character, motivated to lead the United States Air Force in service to our nation." In addition to the Academy's role as a leadership laboratory, it also serves to develop the character of cadets. As I reflect on my experience at the Air Force Academy, I can't help but acknowledge the profound effect their leadership development training had on me. Along the way I learned a lot about the science of leadership and its relationship to character.

Just recently, the Academy finished building the Center for Character and Leadership Development (CCLD). It's a huge architectural glass structure nicknamed Polaris Hall, because it's in the shape of an aircraft rudder that points towards the North Star. Many of us realize the importance of character, but few people actually work consciously on developing and growing their own character. The CCLD aspires to be the center of character development for leaders across the world. That's how important the Air Force perceives character to be for the future of human civilization; leaders have far more influence if they also embrace character.

Not long before graduation at the Air Force Academy, the Firsties (seniors) receive their training assignments for post-graduation. That's when I found out I would be headed to pilot training. It was really happening! All my hard work to that point—all those years of study and effort—had taken me to this moment. It was an exceptional bonding moment for all of us. In just a few short years, we would be flying airplanes for our country.

A few weeks later, as the realization of going to pilot training was still taking root, the female Firsties in my squadron received a unique invitation. Three female officers invited the women in our squadron to meet off base at a local coffee shop. There were only about six of us Firstie ladies, and although we had never received an invitation like this before, we were eager to hear what these female leaders had to say. They had already experienced what we were about to go through in pilot training, and we knew it would be wise to learn from their experiences.

## The Female Factor

About ten women circled around pushed-together coffee tables that evening. The three officers who organized the meeting were already pilots. I'm not sure if they were asked to meet with us by Air Force leaders or if they took it upon themselves to provide us with the personal mentoring opportunity, but I think it was the latter. They seemed genuinely interested in sharing with us some things they had learned as female officers and pilots.

The discussion started off with suggestions on how to manage being both an Air Force pilot and wife and mother. Air Force regulations prohibit female fighter pilots from flying while pregnant, and a nine-month career pause could drastically impact a flying career. Our discussion that night covered many things, such as how to handle professional male/female relationships as an officer, leadership opportunities and hang-ups unique to female leaders, and the new responsibilities we would take on as commissioned officers. There was one topic that stood out in my mind above the rest; all three female officers agreed that we should seriously consider freezing our eggs for future use, and they strongly urged us to do so.

Prior to this meeting, I had endured a series of rigorous 400-level science courses as part of my major in Biology—but no part of our curriculum had anything to do with freezing human eggs. Even so, these women spent a good twenty minutes discussing the science behind saving viable ova for the future and the growing need for professional women to consider it.

This reproductive option is a serious consideration for career women who anticipate delaying childbirth until later years when the ovum may not be as viable. I was struck by their candid tone as well as their boldness for suggesting such a thing to a very vulnerable audience. It was almost like they were giving us a sales pitch for something they wanted us to invest in.

I never elected to freeze any of my eggs. I did have friends who elected to do so, but there was something about the idea that didn't connect with me emotionally. To this day, I have found that the topic is still not widely discussed in military circles; at least among men. On one hand, I imagine the topic is just too personal, but it could also be that the military simply doesn't want to take an official position on such an ethical issue. Either way, it's my opinion that both male and female leaders need to take female issues such as these into consideration, and not just relegate them to coffee house conversations. A significant takeaway from our meeting with these senior officers was the importance of women being willing to lead conversations on women's issues, especially for those who are following in our footsteps.

## Character Development

Looking back at life after my graduation, it was easy to see that my four Academy years were the best four years of my life to that point, but they were also the most challenging ones I had ever experienced. I loved the challenge, I loved the camaraderie; I did not love the high intensity of the program. Although these were the best four years of my life, I would never want to relive them. It seemed like every hour was scheduled with a critical activity; slackers were dealt with, the weak were weeded out.

In the end, the Academy was a good fit for me. On day one, every cadet takes the same Honor Code oath:

*"We will not lie, steal, or cheat nor tolerate among us anyone who does."*

In addition, we were all required to memorize and live by the Air Force core values:

*"Integrity first, service before self, and excellence in all that we do."*

Those core values were modeled for me in my youth, but after four years at the Air Force Academy, they are forever embedded in the fabric of who I am. My personal test of character, the true character I want to be known for, will come from living those values until the day I die. These values define me, and they define what I expect from others around me. They sound right, they feel right, and they stand up to scrutiny.

Once I graduated from the Academy, it was disappointing to discover that many people in our country don't live by or respect these same values. Later in my life, I was shocked to encounter so many public servants who disregard these fundamental principles or espouse them in public but discard them when no one is watching.

June 1st, 2005 was definitely a day to remember. On that day, 922 of us threw our hats into the air in a spectacular expression of excitement and relief and graduated from the Air Force Academy as commissioned officers in the United States Air Force. One of the most rewarding parts about graduating from the Air Force Academy was finishing with a Bachelor of Science Degree and joining the very select group of leaders who can say that they survived one of the most prestigious and grueling universities in the United States.

I will always cherish the lifelong connections I made with hundreds of friends who were classmates in demanding conditions, stress, physical strain, and also hilariously fun times. The men and women who did thousands of pushups and completed the obstacle course at Jack's Valley together became my brothers and sisters. They are the ones for whom I would sacrifice my life; they exemplify the kinds of people who strengthen the framework of America and give life to the definition of freedom. There is no doubt in my mind about the sisterhood and brotherhood of our shared values. Each of them is a life-long friend. As the years have passed some of these friends are no longer with us, having already made the ultimate sacrifice in the line of duty for their country.

Curiously Strong

# *Part Two: Living Curiously Strong*

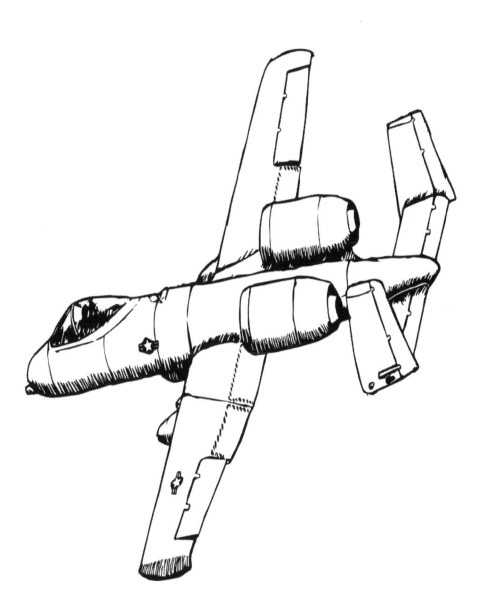

**liv· ing** (2)

Verb

    1.  the pursuit of a lifestyle of the specified type.

**cu· ri· ous· ly**

Adverb

    1.  in a way that shows eagerness to know or learn something.

**strong**

Adjective

    1.  intellectually powerful; able to think vigorously and clearly

    2.  powerfully made or built; tough.

# Chapter 11

## Taking Flight

Of the 922 USAFA graduates who tossed our hats into the air that first day of June, 522 of us were selected to continue on to pilot training. We were divided into classes of about 30 and given orders to pilot training bases throughout the United States. Once at those bases, we were to be joined by other pilot candidates from ROTC and Air National Guard units.

My first exposure to flying an engine-powered aircraft occurred after graduation in a sleek, sporty, single-engine DA-20. The Air Force had started a new program called Introduction to Flight Training (IFT). Evidently there had been a trend of students showing up to pilot schools who were not able to complete the training due to some lack of basic skills. The IFT program was developed to provide both preliminary training and screening of applicants, thus ensuring a greater chance of success for pilot candidates. IFT was a twenty-hour flight program that I completed in Colorado Springs, and I have to say, flying along the Front Range of the Rocky Mountains was a spectacular way to start my flying career.

After my first few hours of flight time, I was very apprehensive about becoming a pilot. Thankfully, I didn't get air sick like some of my classmates, but the smell of aviation gasoline at six in the morning was enough to make me queasy.

Flying can be complicated, and some of my first flights were downright intimidating. There were so many switches and gauges and knobs that did so many things. We had to know which ones did what and when each one was used.

It was interesting wondering about who would ultimately become the better pilots. Some thought athletes would be better, while others thought that the profoundly smart, straight-A students would be the best. My assumption was that anyone who had previous flight experience would rise to the top. Surprisingly, it turns out there is no particular subgroup that is better at piloting than others. Flying is a unique and peculiar skill that can only be mastered with lots of practice.

Once I overheard an instructor make a comment: "Anyone can learn to fly; it just takes different amounts of time for each person." I completely agreed with that sentiment, but the Air Force made it absolutely clear that if you couldn't learn the required skills within a certain number of flights, you would be removed from the flying program. Needless to say, the pressure was on. I needed to develop a completely new skill set in a short amount of time. In the end, the thrill of learning how to fly outweighs all the stress. I would strongly encourage everyone to try it.

The first challenge of the training program was memorizing huge amounts of information. Information like oil pressure or engine temperatures limitations were tested with daily quizzes.

The second main challenge was learning how to multi-task while airborne. We learned this simple mnemonic and repeated it constantly: "aviate, navigate, communicate." These three words serve as a reminder for prioritizing actions in the cockpit throughout a pilot's career. If you get behind in anything else, the most important thing you should do is make sure you are flying the aircraft in a safe manner—aviate. When the aircraft is flying safely, then worry about where you are going—navigate. And lastly, make sure other aircraft and air traffic controllers know your plan—communicate.

That simple mnemonic also serves as a checklist, and it can be applied to other aspects of our lives. When you are stressed out just remember: Keep things safe, figure out your next step, and let others know.

**Keep things safe, figure out your next step, and let others know.**

The third major challenge of the program was learning how to work with fellow classmates. Ultimately, we were competing against each other, but we were also part of a team. We had to be competitive enough not to be last at anything, but cooperative enough that we helped whoever was trailing in performance catch up to the team.

Curiously Strong

## Chapter 12

## *New Jet, New Day*

As I neared the end of my twenty hours of training in that small, single-engine DA-20, I was actually starting to enjoy it. After successfully completing the IFT program, my next training course required that I report to Laughlin Air Force Base in Del Rio, Texas. It was there that I would start *real* pilot training. I had heard stories that pilot training would be the most difficult thing I'd ever done in my life. After I had just spent four years at one of our nation's top-tiered military academies, I was ready to give it my all. That was a good attitude, because the stories I had heard hadn't been exaggerated.

Thirty of us showed up on day one, ready for the challenge, but also ready to compete for the top slot. In my class of thirty there were only two women. The remaining twenty-eight were smart men that I'm proud to call friends and brothers. Most of them had dreamed of being pilots since they were old enough to walk, and most of them didn't just want to be pilots; they wanted to be fighter pilots.

The process of getting selected to fly fighters was multi-faceted. It included being a good pilot, being well respected among your classmates, and then getting selected by Air Force leaders to move into the track of training specifically designed for flying fighter aircraft.

The first step laid out for us was incremental and consisted of two major blocks of 6-month "Phases" of *Undergraduate Pilot Training* (UPT). We would all learn to fly the same basic trainer aircraft, the T-6 Texan II, in Phase I, then progress to flying more advanced trainer aircraft in Phase II or "wash out" of the flight-training program. After six months of flying the T-6 at Laughlin during Phase I, our class would be ranked based on our individual flying performance in the T-6, and sent to Phase II training in other specialized trainer aircraft. We would only finally train in the combat-coded aircraft we would end up flying during our careers if we survived both UPT training Phases I and II first.

Phase II of undergraduate flight training consisted of four possible specialized tracks. The first was for helicopters. One or two people from our class would go on to Fort Rucker, Alabama and learn how to fly helicopters alongside the Army's helicopter pilots. The second track was training in a T-44 turboprop trainer, which would lead in to learning to fly the C-130 "Hercules," a 4-engine turboprop transport aircraft. Five to ten students from our class would be selected to fly the T-44 trainer aircraft at Corpus Christi, Texas.

The largest group of pilots from Phase I would be selected for the third track, to fly the medium-range, twin jet-engine T-1 Jayhawk trainer aircraft, which would ultimately lead pilot graduates to jet-engine transport or refueling aircraft such as C-17s, KC-10s, or KC-135s. The fourth, most coveted track was the T-38 Talon track, leading to all Air Force fighter/bomber pilot assignments. We were told that only the top four or five pilots from our class would be selected for this track, to ultimately become fighter or bomber pilots.

On day one of pilot training, the tension in the room was palpable, as almost everyone in our class wanted to go the T-38 route. Over the next six months we were each put to the test in multiple ways. Air Force regulations dictated that our maximum duty time was 12 hours a day, so we worked 12-hour days, five days a week. During those six months, every flight, every simulator, every classroom assignment, and every ground-training event was graded, and all our scores were compiled. Those performance-based scores were then combined with peer rankings and instructor input. Taking all of that into consideration, the squadron commander would make the final decision on which track each student pilot would be awarded.

Because it was much cheaper to learn certain skills by flying on the ground in a simulator rather than flying aloft, we had more simulator flights for graduation requirements than anything else. The simulators were quite remarkable in that they provided fairly realistic training environments. We could make more mistakes in the simulators, but the simulator instructors, who were primarily retired Air Force pilots, were much less forgiving than our air instructor pilots. The huge, industrial-sized, air-conditioned bays that housed the simulators were also dark and smelly. The stress of learning instrument approaches can induce great amounts of sweat, and the stench of all that flight suit sweat was infinitely worse than some gyms I've been in. Suffice it to say that simulator trainings were everyone's least favorite.

Fortunately, the simulators themselves were more forgiving of mistakes because you wouldn't actually die. Unfortunately, if you did do something wrong, even accidently, you could get a "red screen of death" display, indicating you had just crashed into the ground or another aircraft. If that happened, the instructor would have to reboot the machine and you would have to start all over again.

When our instructor would hit the restart button, he would often say, "New Jet, New Day," as the simulator rebooted. We heard those words so much that my class chose that phrase to be on our class patch. It served as a constant reminder that no matter how badly you mess up, tomorrow will present a new

**No matter how badly you mess up, tomorrow will present a new opportunity.**

opportunity—always good to remember. I caused the simulator to flash my share of "red screens of death," but I literally took life one day at a time and kept learning along the way.

## Choosing the Right Fit

At the end of Phase I, we needed to submit our preferences for which training track we wanted for Phase II. Unlike many of the guys in my class, I had not dreamed of being a fighter pilot. I felt more of a calling to help people, so it was difficult for me to decide what track I wanted. As a result, I spent a lot of time contemplating which aircraft I wanted to spend my career flying.

In making that decision, I fondly remembered some of the stories I heard in my military strategic studies class at the Academy. When troops on the ground were pinned down by the enemy, the number one plane troops on the ground called on for help was the A-10 Thunderbolt II, because it brought with it a huge gun and the "sound of freedom." I felt that flying an A-10 would be an excellent opportunity to help our

Soldiers on the ground. It agreed with who I am at the core; a defender. At the end of our T-6 training I felt called to serve others, so I decided "T-38 fighter pilot training" was the right fit and my first choice for Phase II training, even though I never imagined I would actually get it. The competition was stiff, but the job seemed right for me in every way.

One of the reasons that I never imagined getting selected to fly T-38s and going on to the fighter track was because I felt somewhat unworthy. It was as if I were an interloper, trespassing on sacred ground. Many of my classmates had fathers and grandfathers who had been fighter pilots, and they had dreamed of being fighter pilots since they were toddlers. They had waited their entire lives for this training and had been groomed from youth to be fighter pilots. It was as if their identity and manhood was all wrapped up in this one profession, and it seemed that some of them would stop at nothing to make their dream a reality.

I observed the other candidates' behavior with interest from the first day. Initially, the guys were very friendly. They tried to get to know me, asking me questions about my family and my favorite hobbies. Then the questions became more personal as they assessed whether I was a threat to their childhood dream. They asked if I wanted to fly fighters and having never really thought too deeply about it my response was innocent enough; I didn't know. Then they would ask other questions, such as how long I planned on staying in the military. They implied that only those who were committed to staying in for twenty years were worthy of flying fighters. Again, I wasn't sure if I was going to stay in past my mandatory 12-year commitment, so my answer was the same: I didn't know. Apparently, my perceived avoidance of answering their questions flagged me as a competitor, so their intimidation techniques increased. Over our six months of training, some of the guys even reverted to flirting—to see if I would open up after being flattered.

When I let it be known that I was interested in fighters and was going to request this track on my dream sheet during the final week of Phase I, the psychological intimidation abruptly intensified. One of my male classmates severely underestimated my inner composition. He presumed that I would be an easier mark than the other male pilots, so he tried to intimidate me away from choosing T-38s to increase his chances of getting selected.

He pulled me aside in the hallway and proceeded to coerce me with a petty shakedown tactic. At first, he pleaded with me about how much he wanted fighters and told me that I wasn't a good fit for the fighter world. Then he motioned for one of his friends to join our conversation. His friend happened to be a member of the Air National Guard, who fell under different training requirements. Based on his Guard unit's mission, he already knew he was on track to fly the C-130. He gently nudged my arm and started whispering to get me to lean in more closely to hear him. He then boldly and arrogantly stated, "If you don't vote for my buddy to get fighters, I'll make sure all of the Guard pilots don't vote for you—and you'll never get it."

That did it! I was infuriated by these dull-witted assumptions and simple-minded manipulations. I was not going to allow my hard work to be stolen from me by these playground bullies, so I immediately went to the one instructor that I knew I could trust—a major who happened to be an A-10 pilot—and asked for a private meeting.

It was rare for a student pilot to request and be granted a special meeting that wasn't flying related, but I think the intensity in my eyes alerted the major that I wasn't going to take "no" for an answer.

I appreciated this instructor's understanding of the situation. He reassured me that the selection process was designed to be completely objective and performance-based, and that the intimidation tactics and threats would not impact my future career as a successful Air Force pilot. His reassurance and understanding lifted the weight off my shoulders. During our meeting, I also found out that his fiancée (now his wife) was a fighter pilot.

Occasionally, I wonder if that major had any say in the final determination of which assignment I received for Phase II. Regardless, I will forever be grateful for his character and optimism. Unfortunately, I have since learned that unethical, self-serving characters among us are fairly common, but to this day, it still surprises me how often they are able to rise through society unchallenged.

The last day of Phase I finally came, and we graduated from flying the T-6 and learned what our track would be for phase two. Right up to the minute we walked across the stage one by one and shook hands with the command's top brass, and they congratulate you on completing the program, we still were in the dark about what assignment we were going to receive. There was a huge projection screen at the back of the stage, and as we were shaking hands with the lineup of dignitaries the image of the type of plane we would be learning how to fly next appeared behind us. The students' families filled the auditorium, and my own family was among them. When it was my turn to be called to the stage, up flashed a picture of a T-38 and there was a bunch of cheering and hollering. Naturally I was on cloud nine; I made it to the fighter/bomber track!

As the ceremony ended, I was expecting to go right out and celebrate with my family, but before any celebration was possible, the five of us who were selected for the T-38 fighter/bomber track were ushered to the back of the room and directed into a small classroom. We were shocked to find out that training for the fighter/bomber students began right then and there.

It seemed needlessly dramatic; families and students from all the other tracks were released immediately to go celebrate, but our families—who had flown thousands of miles for our big day—were left wondering what happened to us. We had been whisked away and sequestered without warning.

It was at that hour that I realized my life had not only taken a new direction, but also a new level of intensity— faster-paced than my previous challenges, which had seemed impossible to top when I had gone through them. It felt similar to my first day at the Air Force Academy, only even more demanding. This new cadre of senior officers gave us orders to modify our uniforms so that we would stand out from the other pilots. We were even given a new vocabulary—words that we should start using, as well as words we should stop using. It really was the beginning of a new chapter in my life. They eventually released us that evening and we did get to celebrate with our families, but it seemed like that was the last breather we got for the next six months.

Curiously Strong

# Chapter 13

## Nearing the Speed of Sound

It was truly an honor to be selected to fly T-38s, but out of the 30 students that were attending T-38 school at the time there were only a few women. In fact, it wasn't until the last few weeks of that six-month training program that another female student arrived. The school was tough, and I know that none of us women got there because of our gender. It was about our accomplishments, our hard work, and the quality of our performance in Phase I.

That said, transitioning from flying the T-6 to flying T-38s was like going from driving a Moped to a Ferrari. My new top speed would be the speed of sound. We weren't ever allowed to break the sound barrier, but we sure got close!

The first days of T-38 training involved an overwhelming amount of academics—a mass rote memorization of all the systems. We had to know the oil pressure parameters, the oil temperature parameters, the engine temperature parameters, all the speed limitations, and all the emergency procedures. To give you an idea of the frenetic academic pace, we had to have all the emergency procedures memorized by the second day of training.

Instructor pilots tested our knowledge of emergency procedures using what are known as "stand up" sessions. At a stand up, all the pilots in our group would be seated in a horseshoe around a conference table, and one of the instructors would give us a scenario that involved some kind of malfunction or problem that might occur during ground ops or while airborne. He would then call on a random student pilot, and order that person to stand up. That student would have to go to the head of the table, stand at attention, and recite the exact procedure for handling that particular emergency situation, and it had to be perfect. There could be no deviation from the emergency procedures book. If the student stated anything incorrectly, used the wrong word, or recited a step out of sequence, the instructor would immediately and sternly say, "Sit down!" He would then order someone else to stand up, and the next student would go to the head of table to recite the appropriate actions.

During a stand-up, your heart is racing. You're nervous. You definitely don't want to fail, because you're only allowed so many failures, and if you exceed that number, you are "washed out" of the program. Through each of the training programs there were always a few who didn't make it. The purpose of stand-ups is to invoke a high-stress situation that students can demonstrate the ability to handle while still "at 1-G"—normal gravity. Accomplishing stand-ups in front of instructor pilots and our peers steeled our nerves and instilled focus, teaching us to think quickly, rationally, and calmly through what needed to be done if a problem occurred while in the jet. It seemed like we were subjected to these highly stressful stand-up sessions nearly every day.

In addition to the academics, they soon had us in T-38 simulators. As I mentioned earlier, it's much cheaper to fly a simulator than a real plane, and you don't actually die when you make a mistake and crash.

Almost every aspect of the transition to the T-38 proved to be very stressful. All the parameters, emergency, and operating procedures had to be learned through brute memorization, hard work, and determination. Another entirely new dimension to the equation was the speeds we were operating at—essentially double the speed that we had become used to. When the speed of the jet doubles, the pace of the necessary tasks to operate it also doubles. The lightening-fast pace of decisions, control panel movements, and instantaneous judgment demands extreme mental clarity and exact physical movements.

Thankfully, my brain finally caught up to the pace of processing things at high speed, except for the landing process. I just couldn't figure out how to land the T-38 at 150 mph, and it was plaguing my thoughts and dreams. There was something unnerving about seeing the ground rush toward me so quickly. It was so unsettling that it caused the hair on the back of my neck to stand up.

Day after day, I couldn't seem to make myself land that jet, no matter how closely I followed what the training manual said. It was frustrating, and embarrassing, and I began to think this might get me kicked out of the program—until I had an instructor offer a small, but valuable piece of advice. He said, "Pretend you are trying to intentionally crash, and then pull up a little at the end." I tried it, and it worked! Instead of crashing, I landed, and after that, landing at that speed seemed to be simple for me.

While training in T-38s, I also learned a whole new kind of flying, formation flying. We often had to fly in a formation, a few inches away from the wingtip of another aircraft. We had learned the basics of formation flying in T-6s, but the level of difficulty increased exponentially in T-38s. Four aircraft would fly a hand's span away from each other's wings at double the speed. The skill was all about perspective, focus, and "wiggling your fingers and toes."

"Wiggle your fingers and toes" is an instructor method of relaxing students; it seems odd at first, to be in one of the most demanding environments imaginable and trying to relax, but it is a critical skill we learned. The consequences of not maintaining positions were catastrophic, so formation flying usually induced great amounts of stress. Stress causes muscles to tighten, which makes precision flying much more challenging and dangerous. I often caught myself holding my breath with flexed muscles. After I had an instructor tell me to gently wiggle my fingers and toes while flying in formation, I was able to let my body relax. Formation flying was difficult to learn, but after getting all the wiggles worked out, it became fun.

We would get up to speeds over 300 mph and "hang on" to the wingtip of the flight lead, with just inches separating our jets. Instead of maintaining the entire aircraft in my field of view, the goal was to focus on two or three distinct features of the other aircraft, and keep them lined up as briefed by the instructors. If I lined up the wingtip light with a specific aircraft marking in the right way, I would always be in the right position. It reminded me of Mel Gibson's famous line in *The Patriot* where he instructed his son to "aim small, miss small."

We also learned instrument flying—being able to fly without the ability to see out the windscreen. Instructors simulated weather conditions by making us fly with special hoods over our helmets, so all we were able to see were the plane's instrument panels. I was learning a lot, but more than anything else, I was building confidence.

There were three female T-38 instructor pilots on the base, one of whom I knew from the Academy. One day I had the opportunity to fly with her, and that was a godsend, because I felt I was having a tough time getting through the training. She had a calm demeanor coupled with complete confidence, and she encouraged me in ways that no other instructor had. I wished I could have flown with her more, because I realized in retrospect I could have learned from her more easily than from some of the hard-nosed, aggressive male instructors.

Although it was tough, I made it through T-38 training and just before our graduation ceremony, I learned that I would indeed be assigned to fly the venerable A-10 Thunderbolt—my first choice, and a legendary air-to-ground attack aircraft! Getting that assignment was the final step toward achieving my goal, and I was glad to invite my family to attend our graduation—the ceremony where I finally received my Air Force "wings," and earned the official designation of Air Force Pilot.

## Dog-Fighters vs. Knuckle-Draggers

Immediately after completing T-38 flight training, I was sent to a three-month course called *Introduction to Fighter Fundamentals* (IFF). It was a continuation of T-38 training specifically for fighter pilots (bomber pilots did not attend), focused primarily on an introduction to air-to-air "dogfighting" tactics. Three-dimensional, air-to-air dogfighting tests your mental acuity and physical stamina, and the intense moments of pulling 6-Gs (six times the normal force of gravity) while looking over my shoulder and trying to stay out of weapons range of the "red-air bandit" aircraft behind me, caused me to sweat profusely. The only part I really enjoyed was getting to the final stages of the fight where each jet is fighting for the best position behind the other, in a race to get to the opponent's 6 o'clock position—the optimum weapons engagement zone.

Usually that fight for position ended up with both aircraft pointed straight upward slowing past stall speed in a "rolling scissors" corkscrew maneuver. My favorite memory of being inverted was when my instructor taught me to use my left hand to push up against the canopy to keep my body tightly in the seat as I maneuvered upside down toward the kill zone.

It wasn't until the last phase of this training that we learned air-to-ground bombing techniques that were more closely oriented to the A-10's primary mission. Unfortunately, some of these instructor pilots were the most machismo-infused pilots I had ever met. They espoused that being an air-to-air "dogfighter" pilot was far superior to any other job in the Air Force—even though no American pilot had been in an air-to-air dogfight since the war in Kosovo 15 years earlier. Their derogatory term for air-to-ground pilots was "knuckle-draggers."

I found these attitudes condescending, arrogant, cocky, and in general extremely irritating; having said that, I also believe that they were exactly the type of warriors that we Americans want flying air-to-air combat—bold, brash, and competitive. I had no desire to attempt to compete with them to be the best dogfighter; if given a choice, I would choose an air-to-ground mission over an air-to-air mission every time. Troops fighting on the ground in the Middle East needed close air support, and I was the right person for that mission. I didn't want to waste my time being distracted from my main goal with dogfighting training, which I would hopefully never use.

## Surviving SERE

After IFF I was sent to another required course for fighter pilot training, called SERE, which stands for Survival, Evasion, Resistance, and Escape. I had overheard friends and colleagues whisper about SERE training since my first days at the Academy, and I was not looking forward to it. SERE is a course that was implemented after World War II to provide Soldiers and Airmen who were at risk of being separated from their units (or being shot down) some basic skills that might allow them to avoid capture and survive in the wilderness. Following Vietnam, a significant portion of the course was honed to focus on conduct as a Prisoner of War (POW)—surviving and resisting while in captivity, and escaping when/if an opportunity presented itself. SERE school starts with a group of students stranded in the wilderness for several days with no supplies. It ends with the inevitable capture of the students, teaching students basic techniques to resist torture and mistreatment likely while POWs, and to be ready to take advantage of any possible

**During extreme distress, a person's true character emerges.**

opportunity to escape. It is intentionally and effectively designed to be an utterly miserable experience.

After our "capture" by the bad guys, the small group I was part of endured POW conditions for days. We learned vital mental and physical skills to keep ourselves alive in case we were ever really captured by an enemy—it was during that grueling training that I was forced to expand my mental toughness and understand the sources of my non-physical strength.

Enemies of every kind will try to manipulate people's minds before physically threatening them. During extreme distress a person's true character emerges—for better or, in some cases, for worse.

Character weaknesses inhibit survival and are often revealed in trying circumstances. SERE made me acutely aware of the importance of a personal belief system based on rock-solid, true principles. Without a firm grasp on the basis of your beliefs, self-doubt can quickly overcome and destroy your psyche. It became my firm belief that developing inner strength is of as much importance as building physical strength, if not more so. After my very brief exposure during SERE training to the mental and psychological challenges a POW must be ready to face in order to survive, I knew I would never stop working to strengthen my mind and tenacity.

## *Chapter 14*

## *The Warthog*

I never had childhood aspirations to fly attack aircraft. Growing up in the United States in the 1990s was a time of relative peace and stability at home, so I did not fully appreciate the need for fighter and bomber aircraft. During the summer of 2001 when I joined the Air Force and headed off for the Academy, there was no Air Force involvement in large-scale conflicts that warranted the use of attack aircraft. September 11, 2001 changed all of that; suddenly we seemed to need everything in our arsenal.

Six years after the Twin Towers fell, I was at the end of my T-38 training, and I made my final decision about which aircraft I wanted to fly. The A-10 Thunderbolt II (more commonly, and affectionately, referred to in the Air Force as the *Warthog)* is arguably one of the most incredible and capable attack aircraft ever made. Although the war on terrorism was shifting to a focus on "winning hearts and minds" and the demand for A-10s in combat zones was declining, I was given orders to attend A-10 pilot training at Davis-Monthan Air Force Base in Tucson, Arizona. There, I fell in love with my first Warthog.

The Department of Defense had already started to draw down the number of A-10s it would maintain in its inventory. It had recently closed the A-10 squadron based in Alaska about the time I completed Undergraduate Pilot Training. In fact, before my T-38 training, there had been a relatively long period of time during which there were no A-10 "slots" awarded to students selected for the Phase II fighter/bomber track. It was a huge surprise when the dry spell broke and an A-10 slot opened up in my T-38 class; and then I was selected.

## The Avenger

The A-10 had originally been built right after the Vietnam War and it was the first airplane to be designed and built around a gun. The gun, known as *The Avenger*, is not just any gun. It is a 30mm seven-barrel Gatling-type hydraulically driven autocannon that is 19 feet long and weighs 4,000 pounds. With one ammunition drum alone, the A-10 can knock out multiple tanks from long distances.

That was going to be an awesome gun to fire, but a few things had to come first. "Hog" training started like all my other flight training programs: first a massive rote memorization of facts, then the simulator, and then finally getting to fly the plane.

There weren't any two-seat Warthogs still in use by the time I got to A-10 school, so I was flying solo from my very first flight. I soon found that the A-10s brakes are quite sensitive; seasoned crew chiefs on the ground can usually tell who the new pilots are by the way they taxi the plane. After some atrocious swerving and brake-checks during my first taxi experience in the Hog, I pulled up to the arming crew at the end of the runway who are responsible for arming the gun and pulling aircraft safety pins before flight. The arming crew chief connected his headset to the aircraft and said over the intercom, "Is this your first day?" The simulator obviously did not prepare us for these subtleties.

After my fourth flight, I finally got to shoot that amazing gun. Let me assure you, there is no feeling in the world quite like that! The barrels of the Avenger are mounted right under the cockpit, and the entire front end of the plane reverberates as they spin and fire, spitting out 50 rounds of 30mm bullets per second. Immediately after trigger release, an automatic cooling cycle rotates the barrels on four separate occasions within a two-and-a-half-minute period. This cooling cycle eliminates potential bullet inaccuracies by preventing the barrel from overheating and melting. During the cooling cycle, a quiet humming noise can be heard in the cockpit, and if you drop your oxygen mask, you can smell the cordite (smokeless gunpowder) lingering in the air.

Viewing this entire process while standing on the ground provides an entirely different perspective. When the plane rolls in and strafes a target, first you see a cloud of smoke coming from the nose of the jet, and then the target on the ground explodes. Only after you see all that does the impressive sound of the A-10 gun firing become audible—because the bullets travel faster than the speed of sound.

In addition to that massive gun, the A-10 carries a diverse mix of other ordinance, such as bombs, rockets, and missiles. We also carried defensive counter-measures such as chaff and flares, which we could use to throw off any anti-aircraft missiles that launched our way. When fully loaded, the Warthog can carry an impressive loadout of 16,000 pounds of bombs and bullets. In 2007, Congress surprised us by voting to spend two billion dollars to upgrade the entire A-10 fleet with new wings and with new technology, including GPS precision-guided bomb capability.

In training, we were taught to identify our target and attack it all in the same pass, then pull up quickly and come back around to attack the target again. The cool thing about an A-10 is that it can do this multiple times with its substantial loiter time and munitions loadout, alternating ordinance as required. And, because the A-10 has unusually quiet engines, it can linger around a battle area for hours and make repeated surprise attacks against the enemy from different axes. Is there any question about why ground troops love to see the A-10 show up?

## Hot Pits & Piddle Packs

Training seemed to be going okay, but then, about a quarter of the way through our six-month training program, we were preparing for long duration flights when an unforeseen problem surfaced that needed resolution.

Up to that point, our average A-10 flights lasted anywhere from one to three hours. But A-10s have the ability to carry additional external fuel tanks, which can greatly extend a flight's duration. In addition, A-10s can conduct air-to-air refueling, which extends flying time even more. As well as being in the air for longer stretches, we also learned "hot-pit" ground refueling operations. Essentially, "hot-pitting" is a quick-turn refueling technique used to refuel on the ground while the engines are still running, allowing pilots to refuel and get back to the fight as quickly as possible when air-to-air refueling is not an option. We would fly until we used up all our internal fuel, return to the base, get refueled while sitting in the plane with the engines running, and then take off again to fly another mission. This allowed for twice the training, but it also put twice the amount of pressure on a pilot's bladder.

To alleviate bladder pressure during long flights, male pilots use what are known as "piddle packs." Piddle packs are small plastic bags with an absorbent chemical inside that turns urine into a gelatinous substance. A typical fighter pilot flight suit has a long, double zipper down the front of it. The double zipper (that is, a zipper that can open from the top or the bottom) makes it easy for male fighter pilots to use piddle packs while inside the cockpit, even during flight. That works great for the guys, but what do the women do?

One day, out of the blue, my squadron commander came up to me at the operations desk and asked me to meet with him in his office. I was instantly on high alert, wondering what was wrong. In the military, getting invited to the commander's office usually isn't a good thing. He closed the door and proceeded to tell me that he had never been the commander of a fighter squadron with a woman pilot before; there was a challenge unique to women that he had never previously considered, but knew was important and wanted to make sure I learned—how to pee while flying the A-10.

He stumbled through several suggestions of techniques he had heard about how other female fighter pilots peed while flying. First, he casually mentioned that he knew of several female F-16 pilots that used a catheter. The F-16's cockpit seat is angled backwards, making it more difficult to use gravity to fill a piddle pack, so allegedly some female pilots preferred catheters.

I cringed internally while maintaining my poker face of optimism. He also suggested that I might use a diaper, stating that he might be able to find an extra diaper I could use if I needed one. Again, I cringed internally, but the idea of a diaper perplexed me more than anything. How would I put it on while flying? Would I wear the diaper under my flight suit all day, or strategically stop by a changing room before any flight for which I anticipated the potential need to relieve myself?

Would I need to start calculating how long my body normally needed to process and then eliminate fluids? The commander mentioned that some women intentionally dehydrated themselves, but he also stated that this was a dangerous option because it affected both mental and physical stamina.

Lastly, he suggested that I go talk to another female A-10 pilot. At the time, there weren't any others at the base, but he knew of one who was no longer in the Air Force who lived nearby. I was instructed to use my day off to go talk with Tammy.

I remember talking with Tammy like it was yesterday. It was so refreshing to get her perspective on flying the A-10, and during my visit with her; I realized I was starving for a female perspective. We had very different flying experiences and perspectives, but just being able to discuss it with someone who understood the unique challenges of being a female in an overwhelmingly male workplace was rejuvenating.

Once Tammy dove into the details on how she peed in the A-10, I started laughing hysterically. In fact, I don't think I laughed so hard during the entire six-month training course. It still boggles my mind how technically advanced our military capabilities are, yet female fighter pilots are still trying to aim their pee into a small plastic bag out there somewhere just beyond their flight suit. I used Tammy's suggestions over the rest of my flying career, but I can assure you that it wasn't pretty. Some of my life's most embarrassing moments involve trying to use piddle packs.

Since I saw Tammy's suggestion only as a partial solution I had to get more creative. Having done several "pond crossings" (a flight over a large body of water, usually an ocean) and knowing that neither the catheter approach nor the diaper were viable options for me, I was going to have to get resourceful!

My mother's childhood skill of sewing her own clothes suddenly became an asset for me. Together we figured out a way to sew a hidden zipper into the undercarriage of my flight suits. Technically, altering the uniform broke Air Force regulations. Later in my career, after flying for 10 hours over the Atlantic and another seven-hour flight over the Mediterranean, I was so glad I didn't settle for the diaper option. I was quite pleased with my creative, resourceful solution. And I appreciated having access to a person who is uniquely skilled, so we could make this little individual marvel happen. Even though the miracle was a simple hidden zipper, it was important to me on many levels.

Curiously Strong

## Chapter 15

## *Never Give Up*

After two years of pilot training and six months into A-10 fighter training, I feared I was in danger of being removed from the A-10 program. Throughout the rigors of the Air Force Academy, the trials of flying the T-6, the exhaustion of flying the T-38, surviving the Introduction of Fighter Fundamentals, and enduring the grueling training of SERE, I had worked hard to be objectively competitive with my peers. I had been successful; I was objectively evaluated through each of those courses, and clearly scored high enough to advance to the next level.

However, as I neared my goal of being an operational fighter pilot, I realized that other subjective factors started to figure into my performance evaluations. This was different, and I began to suspect that some of this might have to do with my gender.

The first thing I noticed was that I wasn't quite as welcome in this unit as I had been in previous units. For instance, some of my colleagues thought it would be funny to deposit their full, leaky piddle packs in my locker. The message was a nasty one. These acts caught me by surprise and left me wondering about the implications.

It didn't help that I was the only female pilot in the squadron. In fact, I was the only female officer in the entire building. The only other women in the building were enlisted, and I was cautioned as a pilot not to get too friendly with them. Thinking back this was probably a good rule for male fighter pilots, but was arbitrarily and mindlessly applied to me, too. The military has a no-fraternization rule that mandates separation of social and personal relationships between officers and enlisted personnel. In practice, this unfortunately turned out to mean that the male pilots in the squadron had their exclusive boy's club, and I was on my own. I felt profoundly isolated.

I am aware that many women work in male dominated organizations. My situation was significantly different. There was no one to go home to at night to relieve the testosterone overload, no roommate, and no close friend to go to dinner with on weekends. This was total and prolonged isolation. It provided a unique opportunity for me to identify exactly what the differences are between male and female behaviors. I was acutely aware of what was *not* present.

Furthermore, I was slowly convincing myself that maybe I wasn't hacking it. My typically high personal standards were not accepted as good enough. I was different than my male peers, and they confirmed those differences daily. I started slipping, making mistakes that appeared serious to my instructors, and their attitude about me also began to change. For example, one of my worst mistakes was during my first four-ship flight for bombing patterns, which consists of four planes flying together in a tight pattern over a target on the ground; two students flying and two instructors. It was very sequential, intense, rhythmic, fast-paced learning and execution. New directions and commands were broadcast over the radio every five seconds.

Keeping my eyes on the three other aircraft in our small square-bombing pattern, I waited for my turn to roll in onto the attack leg to drop my ordinance. I was supposed to drop a bomb—initiated by pressing the red "pickle button" on the control stick with my thumb. But I had become what is often referred to as "task-saturated," and instead of moving my thumb to press the pickle button, my trigger-finger squeezed the trigger of the gun. The Avenger spat out 50 rounds-per-second, and then I pulled up into the recovery pattern, just like I was supposed to. With my brain focused on everything going on around me in the pattern, it took me several seconds to realize I had used my index finger instead of my thumb.

Approximately five seconds later, about the same time I realized my mistake, a voice came over the radio: "Did you know you fired your gun?"

I responded, "Yes."

The training was stopped immediately and we all flew back to the base. I had "hooked" the flight—meaning I had failed.

Once we were out of our planes, I was prepared for the onslaught of criticism for making a mistake. I was shocked when they asked if I had planned to lie about my mistake. Apparently, the instructors were concerned that I hadn't "fessed up' to the mistake on the radio as soon as I made it. I had had five whole seconds to say something, and despite the fact that it had taken those seconds for my brain to catch up to the situation and realize I'd messed up, they alleged I might have been planning not to say anything, hoping no one would notice.

They did not know me or understand who I was and had jumped to conclusions, which then escalated to accusations.

To the instructors, this was a question mark on my integrity, a character flaw. Regardless of my intention to say something once I realized my mistake, the fact that there was five seconds of silence followed by someone asking me if I fired my gun was enough to put doubt in their minds and they jumped on it.

It was unfathomable to me that my honest training mistake resulted in a question of my integrity. The mistake was bad enough, but now my actual mistake was being ignored, and instead an entirely different accusation of lack of integrity was fabricated, of which I was not guilty.

Whenever a pilot "hooks" a flight, the training exercise must be flown again to prove the pilot won't make the same mistakes or can demonstrate proficiency in the required tasks. This is a relatively common occurrence in pilot training and happened several times to student pilots in previous programs, and a few times to other student pilots during my A-10 training course as well. I successfully passed my next ride, but this one incident seemed to provide a reason for instructors to put me under the microscope. After that, it seemed I was perceived as the weakest link; a liability they were intent on eliminating.

From that day forward, every instructor I flew with gave me a piece of his mind about how I wasn't quite cutting it. In the meantime, my male classmates all came back from their sorties, confidently boasting about "shacking the target," or hitting a bullseye, every time. As I listened to their successes and noted that most of their flights seemed to be unscathed by mistakes documented by their instructors, I quietly wondered if perhaps God had a different plan for me. Still, I didn't understand how I could have made it all the way through two years of pilot training, where my abilities had served me well, only to suddenly fail on the final stretch.

## The Quest for Rhinoceros-Thick Skin

As training progressed, sexual innuendos and explicit comments started to intensify. It became customary for the men around me to use vulgar language about body parts and body functions. Their sly comments often seemed to have double meanings, and any time they could make a coarse comment out of otherwise innocent conversation, they seemed to jump at the opportunity. I had witnessed that kind of joking and crude, juvenile behavior before, but it became so frequent that it started to wear on me. They say one of the steps in becoming a good fighter pilot is developing thick skin. I felt isolated, but my skin was getting thicker by the day, whether I wanted it to or not.

Even though I was trying to be resilient, being the only woman in a fighter squadron was not easy. It took a lot of sweat, strain, endurance and fortitude to hang on to my faith in the fighter pilot world, but eventually I came to the realization that in general, women are not trained to recognize and voice these behaviors as wrong, or taught the necessary skills to handle the unique aspects of working in traditional all-male environments. Conversely, in general, men in male-dominated organizations are not taught or trained to recognize females as assets to their organizations, or taught the skills needed to work side by side with females successfully. I now believe that when men and women work together, we all benefit from what the others bring to the table, and the end-product is superior to single-gender operations.

Another complication during A-10 flight training was that one instructor refused to fly with me because he didn't want to fly with a woman. He claimed to be unable to instruct me because he didn't understand my learning style as a woman. While I thought it was a poor excuse to get out of doing his job, I also thought he was perhaps actually being the most honest of the bunch. His refusal ended up being a blessing in disguise; he was very hot-tempered, and my ability to learn when he became loud and volatile was essentially squashed.

I was not the only pilot making mistakes, but it still seemed as though my performance continued to receive an imbalanced proportion of scrutiny. It also seemed that bias was creeping into some of the grading. One day, we were training on a low-altitude sortie, which meant that while we had to fly quite low, we still needed to remain at least 500 feet above the ground. While flying the jet along at 400 miles per hour, I dropped down to 500 feet. While there, I unintentionally dipped ten feet below the minimum altitude, to 490 feet. This can happen to any pilot, and a few seconds later I corrected my altitude, but my instructor determined I hadn't corrected it fast enough, and that it was a hook'able offense. That meant I would have to repeat the entire two-hour flight, to ensure I did not make that mistake again.

Student pilots were allowed to hook three sorties throughout the program. Small mistakes here and there were also considered unavoidable, but if we made three mistakes that an instructor determined were hook'able offenses, students were required to fly the next flight with the squadron commander, and he would evaluate student performance to determine whether the student should be allowed to continue in the program. That 10-foot flying error resulted in my third hooked flight, and even though I successfully passed my next flight with the squadron commander, he seemed to hold a disproportionate number of instructor meetings about my potential inability to hack it. This may have been a motivational method he had used to good effect in the past with his male students, but it was counter-productive with me. I resented his perceived attempts to publicly shame me into better performance, but I got through it by relying on the stoic acceptance I had cultivated throughout my training.

The criticism was harsh and aggressive. The pressure was enormous. Every bomb and bullet that we dropped or fired during training was graded for error and distance from the target and I was being given every signal that I was not succeeding.

I was feeling alone and under tremendous pressure, but failing wasn't an option for me, so I refused to give up. It just isn't in my blood. I had spent my life setting and achieving goals, so I showed up each day with a tighter jaw, and thicker skin. The other pilots seemed confident they were getting everything right, and boasted about their successes; I was sure nothing was going well, so I kept my mouth shut and drilled down within myself to find areas where I could do better. Along the way, I managed to strengthen my inner resolve; I would not quit.

At the end of A-10 training, I was glad to officially and successfully complete my final check ride. This certainly had not been my best training experience; I was grateful just to be graduating.

## *Top Gun*

When graduation day came, the ground crew set one of our hangars up for the festivities. They even polished an A-10 until it looked like it had been spit-shined, to use it as the back-drop for our graduation ceremony. That impressed me, because as fighter planes go, the A-10 is fairly ugly and its paint job is dull by design and somewhat visually unappealing—it didn't get the name "Warthog" for nothing. The maintenance personnel hadn't let that stop them though, and I was quietly amazed that they had worked so hard to get the aircraft ready and the hangar set up, for just seven of us to graduate.

I timidly stood next to my classmates at the front of the hangar by the A-10, thankful to have made it through the rigorous challenge. I was eager to receive my certificate of completion and move on to my first operational fighter unit. I too had been convinced that my performance was less than optimal. I was so embarrassed, I specifically asked my parents not to attend the graduation ceremony, but since many of the other pilots' families and friends were in attendance it was standing room only.

The simulator instructors were all retired A-10 pilots, and they stood along the back wall. Throughout my training, they had seemed to doubt my abilities even more than the active duty instructors. I understood their skepticism: they had made it known during training that they had never served with female A-10 pilots.

The room drew quiet as the ceremony began, and the Group Commander stepped forward to present the awards. The three most notable awards were Distinguished Graduate, Top Academic, and the much-coveted Top Gun award. The Top Gun award was completely objective and clearly mathematical. It went to the pilot whose bombs and bullets hit the targets closest to the bullseye throughout the entire training course.

In the weeks leading up to graduation, I had overheard some of my classmates comparing notes on whom they thought would win Top Gun. Some of them kept meticulous notes on how well they were scoring on their bombing runs. Still, nobody knew for sure who was going to win it. As for me, I never kept track of my scores. I had decided months earlier that my only goal was simply to survive in order to graduate; I wasn't concerned about my name being on an award.

During the ceremony, I had taken a place standing at the end of the row of pilots. The idea was to be inconspicuous, graduate, and slip away. As the ceremony progressed, the Distinguished Graduate and the Top Academic award winners were announced, and there was the usual applause. But you could have heard a pin drop in that hangar after *my* name was announced as winner of the Top Gun award.

I quickly looked back and saw the faces of the simulator instructors standing at the back of the room. Their jaws had dropped. My jaw had dropped. I looked back at my commander and instructors, and I uttered a sincere question out loud, "Is this a joke?" I thought for sure that they had conspired to rib me one last time before I left.

It was no joke. I had actually won Top Gun.

I still wish to this day that I could see the results of all the bombing and shooting runs we did. I'd love to learn by how much of a margin I out-shot my classmates.

## Chapter 16

## Sweet European Dreams

My first operational assignment in the A-10 Warthog took me on a life-changing adventure to Spangdahlem Air Force base in Germany, not far from the Belgium and Luxembourg borders. Other than travels to and from Israel at the age of ten, I had never traveled through Europe. My opportunity came when I had just turned 25 and the Air Force bought me a one-way ticket to Ramstein, Germany. Having just gotten out of school and landed the career of a lifetime, I felt certain that I had finally "arrived" at adulthood; and I spent three of the most adventure filled years of my life living in Europe.

Not long after I arrived, I rented a small house near the Mosel River in the village of Salmtal, about a 20-minute drive from the base. My landlord's name was Wolfgang, and he was the nicest landlord I've ever had. He told me he liked renting to Americans because he could earn more money on rent, and Americans tended to keep his house cleaner.

I loved the countryside. It reminded me of living in rural Idaho, and I would often go for walks when I wasn't at work. One of my neighbors was a dairy farmer, and every week I walked over to his dairy to get a quart of fresh milk. His English was not very good, but we managed to have some interesting conversations. Before long, I volunteered to help him milk the cows. It was something else that reminded me of living in Idaho.

The wet weather in Germany created a difficult flying environment, because it required more instrument flying, and we practiced it a lot. I logged more instrument flying there than in any other country, but when the clouds broke and the sun was shining down on all those green fields, flying in Germany was absolutely beautiful. Since the airbase wasn't far from the Rhine River, when we got back from a mission early enough we would get the treat of being able to fly along the river and enjoy the sight of all of the amazing medieval castles and fortresses.

**Despite the danger, flying the line between the water and the sky was absolutely exhilarating.**

Through the Status of Forces Agreement, each country in NATO set forth the parameters we were required to follow during our practice flights, and depending on where we were flying, we would have to spend a lot of time jumping through hoops. One of the training ranges where we liked to go was on an island off the coast of the Netherlands; the paperwork to fly there was minimal, and we would practice low-level attacks and drop training ordinance into a sand pit that was shaped like a bullseye.

Our approaches to the target there were usually just a few hundred feet above the surface of the water, so whenever we flew those attack runs, my awareness of every slight movement I made was instinctively heightened. Barely being able to differentiate between the blue sky and blue water while looking out the front windscreen was an eerie feeling, and at that low altitude, one tiny mistake, or accidental input to the flight controls, could be catastrophic. Despite the danger, flying the line between the water and sky was absolutely exhilarating.

During my time in Germany, we had the opportunity to fly over many parts of Europe, and even the Middle East. During one mission, we were sent out to retrieve some A-10s that had been flown hard in the Iraq and Afghanistan wars, and needed to return to a permanent maintenance base for overhaul. The maintenance had to be conducted outside of the war zone, so I and a small group of other pilots volunteered to transport them back to the maintenance depot. We were flown to a rendezvous point in the desert, where we picked up our A-10s and headed back.

## Got the T-Shirt

One night during the long, multi-day trip back, we stopped at a Forward Operating Base to fill up on fuel and get some rest. I was apparently dealing with jet lag, because at 2:00 a.m. I was still awake. That particular base had some basic facilities, so I decided to go to the gym to work off some energy after sitting all day in the cockpit of an A-10.

When I entered the gym building, I noticed a flier on the wall. It was encouraging people to stay in shape by lifting weights, and there was an incentive: If a lifter could bench press 150 pounds, they would get a free t-shirt with the base logo on the front. I jumped at the idea of getting a free souvenir just for practicing my weight-lifting abilities, so I did a quick warm-up and headed into the weight room.

It was the middle of the night, so the weight room was nearly empty. There was only one other Airman working out. I thought about asking him to be a spotter, but I knew the weight would be light enough that I wouldn't need one. I did several warm-up sets before I lifted the required amount several times just to make sure I wouldn't embarrass myself. Then I went to the front desk and asked the young lady monitoring the facility if I could do the lift to get the free shirt. She was hesitant, but agreed.

She walked with me back into the weight room and looked around sheepishly. She commented, "You are going to need a spotter for safety reasons, and I can't do it since that is a lot of weight." Then, almost like it had been staged, a voice came from across the room. It was the Airman who had been working out. In a loud commanding voice, he said, "She doesn't need a spotter; she just lifted that ten times!" I grinned from ear-to-ear. The young lady shrugged her shoulders and proceeded to let me complete the bench press without a spotter. I received my free t-shirt, and then headed off to get a good night's rest.

The next morning, it didn't take my fellow pilots long to notice my new t-shirt. They asked me how and where I got it, so I shared the story. I had no idea that story would eventually be used to help determine my fighter-pilot call sign.

## What's in a Name?

The tradition of fighter pilots having call signs, or nicknames, goes back to the early days of air warfare. Historians tell us that call signs helped people on the ground and in the air keep track of who was who when flying. You can imagine the confusion if three different pilots in a squadron all had the same name. As for how pilots get their call sign, it often has to do with a play on the pilot's name, a flyer's personality traits, or something the pilot does that stands out to other pilots—usually some kind of mistake or "buffoonery."

The first time I asked a fighter pilot how he earned his call sign, he assertively informed me that I would have to buy him a beer before he would tell me. It was, shall I say, nothing I should repeat here. That was the last time I ever asked a male fighter pilot how he got his call sign. Some fighter pilots will tell you the meaning behind their call sign only if they know and trust you, ultimately revealing that you are truly a friend if they share such a personal story.

I had been told that I would not earn a call sign until I had gained approval by other fighter pilots in my operational flying unit; they would assess me for several months and wait for me to do something "dumb, dangerous, or different." Immediately thereafter, they would hold a naming ceremony.

Naming ceremonies are interesting events. During the ceremony, the other fighter pilots in the person's operational flying unit gather in a room at the squadron or perhaps the Officer's Club. The person being named cannot be in the room. Once they convene, fellow pilots begin telling stories about the person about to be named, usually ones that are perhaps "ten percent truth," to make the stories as entertaining as possible. Tradition mandates that only after all stories have been told and a consensus on the call sign has been reached, should the person to be named be allowed to enter the room to receive their call sign.

To be sure, from the time I arrived in Germany I had been using extra caution to not do anything "dumb, dangerous or different" in fear that I might end up with a bad call sign. Being the only woman in the squadron made me feel that I was starting with a disadvantage, and that did not bode well for a potential name.

It wasn't long after we brought those A-10s back to Germany for maintenance that the other pilots in my unit held a naming ceremony for me. Obviously, I was a bit nervous—you never know what fighter pilots are going to come up with. I was relieved to find out that my name wasn't based on anything I did that was dumb. It turned out that getting my free t-shirt rekindled talk about my weightlifting reputation, and my fellow fighter pilots decided I should be called "Altoid," because, just like the advertising slogan on the tin of mints says, I was "curiously strong."

## *Chapter 17*

## *Bulgarian Buddies*

Throughout my time in Germany we conducted regular training to stay combat qualified. The term for this is "maintaining currency," and one of the requirements was to fly at least nine sorties each month. This practice also kept the jets finely tuned, because if we noticed something wasn't working quite right, it got immediate attention.

As I previously mentioned, through the Status of Forces Agreement we were authorized to use training facilities in other countries, and to drop dummy rounds on their ranges. We usually dropped training ordinance in Germany, Luxemburg, and the Netherlands. I also got the opportunity to shoot live AGM-65 Maverick missiles, designed for close air support, at dummy targets—old boats—off the coast of England. None of it was frivolous; we took our training seriously and appreciated the opportunity to learn from the release of every bomb and bullet. My appreciation for these excellent training opportunities, possibly the best pilot training in the world, grew even deeper when we participated in a month-long exercise in Bulgaria.

During this exercise, we conducted weeks of flying and training with Bulgarian SU-25 Frogfoot pilots. The *Frogfoot* is the Russian equivalent of the A-10 and is often referred to as the "flying tank." As Bulgaria was an old Soviet Bloc country, their military fleet was comprised primarily of older Soviet aircraft.

Even though the Frogfoot was designed and built around the same period as the A-10, you couldn't tell so by looking at the two aircraft side-by-side. Granted, I'm a little biased, but after looking at a Frogfoot, you might have assumed it had been towed in from the nearest junkyard. It was apparent that their maintenance crews had vastly fewer resources to maintain their jets than our US crews did ours. I was even more shocked to learn that Bulgarian pilots were able to fly their planes only a few times each year.

Sitting in the cockpit of a Frogfoot and trying to decipher the controls was a cultural smorgasbord. The instruments were labeled in Russian, the GPS was in English, and the ordinance system was labeled in Bulgarian. I'm still not sure where the red button to employ weapons was located.

After we got airborne with the Bulgarians to practice our bombing runs, my eyes were opened even more. In American training, we are scored by how many inches or feet we are off from our intended targets. I was shocked to see the Bulgarian pilots regularly miss their ground targets by *hundreds* of feet.

To me, this experience was a dramatic demonstration of the importance of keeping our American military well-trained and well-funded—especially if we are serious about keeping our country safe and secure. It made me proud that no matter where I went in Europe, the US pilots seemed better trained, and our aircraft were better maintained.

Spending the month in Bulgaria also revealed the marked differences that occur in the landscape and the communities within a different government structure.

Our hotel accommodations were nearly thirty miles from the base where we trained, so each day I spent a couple hours gazing at the countryside from the inside of a van. The countryside of Bulgaria is beautiful; the areas in between the country's small villages contain massive fields of roses and other flowers. One small town was completely different from the rest, with their laundry draped throughout their yards, and small animals such as goats and sheep roaming freely, reminding me of Middle Eastern towns. It was a town of Romani, known, as "Roma," or sometimes pejoratively referred to as Gypsies. Our Bulgarian guides suggested we not stop near the village, due to a lack of security in the area.

In Bulgaria's larger towns, I noted a distinct absence of individual homes; there were no "neighborhoods." Instead, the landscape was filled with high-rise buildings that were built during the Cold War. Most of the apartment buildings were in dreadfully poor condition, and much infrastructure seemed dilapidated and crumbling. It was almost as if no maintenance had been accomplished in the last 50 years.

On the plus side, even though Bulgaria had just become part of the European Union, they were still maintaining their own currency. That meant that the price of goods had not skyrocketed like in other European countries, and I was delighted that I could buy an extremely large scoop of ice cream for only one American dollar.

The air base where we trained also suffered from a crumbling infrastructure, and at times, training proved to be challenging. The runway was not in the pristine condition we were accustomed to seeing; instead of a solid asphalt surface, the runway consisted of concrete pavers linked together, and there were some wide cracks. That made for bumpy takeoffs and landings.

Throughout this training in austere conditions, I was impressed with our American maintenance personnel who remained dedicated to keeping our A-10s ready and flying no matter what the circumstances were. I suspected we would soon need lots of new tires since the runway was so rough.

## A Patriotic Spirit

From the beginning of my time as a pilot, my favorite part of any flying squadron was the maintenance crew chiefs. They put their sweat and pride into making sure each plane was safe to fly, and they took satisfaction in knowing that the ordinance they loaded could accurately hit the target. Each pilot often spent only a couple hours a day in the cockpit, but the crew chiefs and back-shop maintainers would spend the rest of each day crawling all over the jets. Their pride in those planes could be seen in the absolute combat readiness of each A-10, and they worked around the clock when aircraft needed maintenance to keep them that way.

When I stepped up to my jet, I looked forward to connecting with the crew chief. We would usually do the walk-around inspection together, often getting a thumbs-up from the other maintenance supervisors who were making their rounds. One day while preparing for a flight in Bulgaria my respect for the ground crew grew even greater.

I had arrived at my jet and was going through my routine inspection and making small talk with the crew chief, when one of the maintenance supervisors walked over from the main hangar. I was curious about his intentions and I stopped my walk-around and greeted him. He had a large Ziploc bag in his hands, and he pulled a perfectly folded American flag and a handwritten list of countries out of it. He told me that he had a personal favor to ask, and he requested that I fly with his flag in the cockpit with me on my mission that day. That flag had been with him throughout his entire Air Force career, and he managed to have it flown in every country where he had served.

> **Patriotism is contagious.**

I was honored to be able to put my name on his list as the pilot flying that flag over Bulgaria. I will never forget that man's soul-deep patriotism; that experience is one of the reasons I fly a flag on my front porch to this day. Patriotism is contagious.

## Historical Impact

Alongside the airbase runway in Bulgaria were rows of Soviet-era hardened aircraft shelters. As I thought about this, I realized it was remarkable to be developing an alliance with people who may have been adversaries just a generation ago but had now become allies and friends. In fact, I think each of their Frogfoot pilots jumped at the rare opportunity to get acquainted with American pilots. Although I was a relatively new A-10 pilot who had not yet earned the complete trust of many of my own colleagues, the Bulgarian pilots instantly befriended me, and they were complete gentlemen. They also seemed spellbound by the fact that I was a *female* fighter pilot.

Many Bulgarians we interacted with knew some English, but none of us knew any Bulgarian. In order to conduct communications necessary to get our training organized, the

> **Significant synergy occurs when women work alongside men.**

local embassy provided a translator. Our translator was a Bulgarian woman named Kalina. I instantly took a liking to Kalina, partly because she was one of the few women on the base, but also because she was full of personality. I also discovered I was eager for her insights and perspectives on many things. Don't misunderstand, I thoroughly enjoyed working with the guys in my squadron, but as at every other assignment, having no female colleagues around was isolating and lonely. The time I was able to spend with Kalina helped reaffirm the enormous value women bring to any work place. Female perspectives have distinct and substantial value, and significant synergy occurs when women work alongside men. As I mentioned before, I've noticed that productivity and effectiveness gaps seem to exist in teams comprised of "just men" or "just women."

Kalina grew up living in an apartment as many in Bulgaria do. Her father was a pharmacist, and it was Kalina's dream to work for the United Nations; when she went to college, she earned multiple degrees in languages and international studies.

I enjoyed getting to know Kalina and spent some time with her almost every day. One thing I quickly learned was that she loved cheese; when she was a child living under communist rule, cheese wasn't readily available. She also refused to sleep in an air-conditioned room. I was puzzled and asked her to explain why; she told me that she had been taught as a child that breathing air-conditioned air could cause serious health problems. In all my studies I had never heard anything to that effect, but she believed it to the core. Later, I learned that in Kalina's youth, the communist government paid for everyone's energy usage. To keep costs down, they published propaganda that discouraged people from using air conditioning. Sadly, even educated people like Kalina believed it.

It's a question some people never consider: "Would a government perpetrate a lie to manipulate its people?" The story Kalina believed about air conditioning wouldn't be the first time propaganda was used to manipulate or control a populace. At the time, I could not imagine growing up in a world where government propaganda influenced my behavior.

Although I was in Bulgaria for less than a month, saying goodbye to Kalina was the hardest part about leaving. When we left, the sadness on her face was evident. As we were saying our goodbyes, I made the common farewell of, "I'll email you and maybe we can meet up again." I remember Kalina laughing as she said, "You Americans are all the same. You write once after a few weeks. Then you write again several months later, and then I never hear from you again."

Her words of truth stung a bit, as I realized she spoke from experience. Americans, or maybe American military personnel, do seem to have a reputation for quickly making new friends and then unmaking friends just as easily. I still stay in touch with Kalina; her observation taught me something about people, and I made the determination to grow from what I learned.

# Curiously Strong

## Chapter 18

## *Reduction in Force*

In 2008, the United States elected a new Commander-in-Chief, and the policies he implemented put a new burden on the Air Force. The longstanding military phrase of "do more with less" began filling our squadrons and offices with increasing frequency.

The amount of funds available for training was reduced drastically, as was the amount of flying we were allowed to do. Careers were also impacted; my Air Force Academy graduation class of 2005 took the initial hit for mandatory "force shaping" operations, another term for "reduction in force." It was mind-boggling to me and many of my fellow Academy graduates. As pilots, we had been required to sign commitments to serve 10 years after our pilot training because of the considerable expense of training; suddenly the Air Force was asking hundreds of us to leave before our ten-year obligations were fulfilled.

I was one of hundreds to receive notification that I might get "force shaped." That letter changed my perspective on my Air Force career. Suddenly, it seemed it might come to an abrupt and unexpected end. I started to plan for that contingency and looked into the options I might have if I were to suddenly become a civilian once again.

Since I had just spent the last three years training to become a pilot, the natural assumption would be that I could become a civilian pilot. That's a common path, but there was a limiting factor; I did not yet have enough hours in an aircraft to get a job as an airline pilot. It was gut wrenching to think that those two years of arduous pilot training could end up being worthless.

There were good reasons to believe the rumors that our A-10 squadron in Germany was going to be shut down, and it eventually was a couple years later. The Air Force had been tasked to reduce its force structure, and that order was being implemented quickly. About the same time that I was pondering my options, a memo arrived at the base. The Air Force was requesting that a pilot from each unit be reassigned to fill a deployment to Afghanistan. The pilot would be retrained to fly another new aircraft—one dedicated to a top-secret mission.

## Birthing Project Liberty

The new Commander-in-Chief had initiated a different perspective on how the wars in Afghanistan and Iraq would be fought. Instead of a "War on Terror," operations shifted toward a more subtle counter-insurgency strategy. Instead of destroying the enemy with military actions, the emphasis shifted to winning the hearts and minds of the indigenous people. This meant we needed fewer fighter aircraft missions and more reconnaissance missions.

To address these changes, the Secretary of Defense created a task force with a very clear focus: recommend solutions for increasing the amount of our Intelligence, Surveillance, and Reconnaissance (ISR) so we could support the two-war situation ongoing in Iraq and Afghanistan. One of the task force's recommendations was Project Liberty, the creation of two squadrons to fly manned, medium-altitude airframes equipped with ISR capabilities.

The airframe they selected for this new mission was the Beechcraft King Air 350. The Air Force purchased 37 of these, augmented them with special Air Force equipment, and then designated the resultant aircraft system the MC-12. The "M" designator referenced the aircraft's "multi-role" capability. Each MC-12 would operate with a four-person crew—two pilots and two systems operators. The program was new to the Air Force, so they needed pilots to fill these vacant roles, quickly.

Project Liberty began pulling individuals from squadrons throughout the Air Force to operate the new platform. Given speculation that my fighter squadron, and likely my beloved A-10, were about to be scrapped, and worried the Air Force would have spent all that time and money training me for no return, I was determined to justify that investment by fulfilling some combat role before I became one of those officers whom the Air Force "no longer needed."

Along with the likelihood of being discharged if I tried to stay in the A-10, it seemed that the flexibility to go where the Air Force needed me and the opportunity to increase my flight time for my eventual civilian future were worth the transition. Both the new experience and the additional hours would be helpful for my career whether I stayed in the Air Force or not, so I jumped at the chance to be one of the new MC-12 pilots. This required me to fly back to an Air National Guard base in Mississippi and be trained in this new airframe. After my training, I climbed aboard a C-17 transport and headed to the war zone in Afghanistan.

Curiously Strong

## Chapter 19

### Touring Afghanistan by Air

During the C-17 flight into Afghanistan, I was immediately fascinated by the landscape. As I peered out one of the side windows, I saw an endless spread of rugged, snow-capped mountains. It almost reminded me of some regions back home in Idaho. What I was looking at is called the Hindu Kush, a chain of mountains that extends 500-miles along the Afghanistan-Pakistan border. Many of the peaks are nearly 17,000 feet high, and one peak tops out at over 25,000 feet. You could tell water was scarce, and that its presence dictated the location of any population centers. The run-off from those snow-capped mountains provided most of the water for the communities nestled in the adjacent valleys.

The evidence of the recent history of the nation chilled me as we flew over the remnants of Russian military equipment that dotted the barren countryside. What's left of the Buddhas of Bamiyan, a World Heritage Site, was in the distance. These were statues of Buddha, carved into the side of a cliff in Bamiyan Valley northwest of Kabul, Afghanistan's capitol city. In 2001, the Taliban used dynamite to destroy this historic site (it is their custom to wipe out pre-Muslim history). In 2006, efforts began to restore the statues, but as I looked out the window of that C-17, it became apparent that the land had not known peace, security, or freedom in many generations.

I arrived at Bagram Air Base in Afghanistan in the fall of 2010. Tucked away in my luggage, I brought with me an ice chest full of German bratwurst, sauerkraut, and mustard to help cheer up those who had been there for a long time. I enjoyed getting to know a huge new diverse group of pilots and operators. We had a wide range of backgrounds and aircraft experiences, and our sharing of our combined knowledge made it easy to learn my new job. It also made the long deployment go by relatively quickly.

## Winning Hearts and Minds

When I first received my deployment orders to Afghanistan, I had never stopped to think about how many women were serving in combat roles. Women were everywhere on those forward-deployed bases, but I also noticed that while serving in combat, women tended to behave differently than they did elsewhere.

First, I was surprised to discover how many single women wore fake wedding rings while serving in combat environments. I learned that the main reason for their deception was to keep the men mission-focused. Deployed men have an uncanny ability to rapidly identify single women, and that can distract them from their responsibilities.

I also noticed that deployed women often chose not to wear makeup—or at least limited the amount of makeup they wore. Many of them chose not to wear makeup because of the hot, dusty environment, but some of them were specifically trying to deter flirtatious men.

I also learned that females were tasked with some unique roles in Afghanistan. The military's Counter-Insurgency (COIN) operations included military, political, economic growth, and community outreach objectives to help deter terrorism. All military branches deployed females in COIN operations, and they often served in roles their male counterparts couldn't.

The Army even initiated a Special Operations Female Engagement Team (FET). Their role was to work specifically with Afghan women and children, teaching them about hygiene and how to make things they could sell. One of the aims of this program was to provide the women with the means to earn a wage and be more independent. Servicewomen also served in irreplaceable roles as translators, screeners, and on cultural support teams.

It was refreshing to see women being recognized for their unique skills and traits, and using those skills in a combat environment. It is also noteworthy that these same FET teams were on the ground filling combat roles prior to 2013, when the US formally lifted its ban on women serving in ground combat roles.

Curiously Strong

## *Chapter 20*

## *The Battle of Do Ab*

Spending countless days flying in circles around the barren and rugged landscape of Afghanistan gave me new appreciation for Bill Murray's character in the movie, *Groundhog Day*. Most of the time, our operations were very monotonous, and many of my missions were conducted under the cover of darkness. This meant I not only had to sleep during the hottest hours of the day, but also that I had to recondition my circadian rhythm. I needed to be fully alert for planning and flying my missions, and then fully asleep while off duty.

Although many nights at work we operated on the verge of library silence, sometimes they were action-packed. One day I walked into the operations room and everyone was abuzz. There were friendly troops on the ground under fire upon by the Taliban; they needed help, and they needed it NOW.

The date was May 25, 2011. An Army scout platoon had been tasked with contacting village elders in Do Ab, a small town in the Nuristan province in the northeastern part of Afghanistan. Two of our Tactical Air Control Party (TACP) operators augmented their team. TACP operators are Air Force personnel who accompany Army combat units. Their role is to provide advice and coordination for any air support needed by the combat unit. (I found out afterwards that one of those TACP operators had previously been assigned to the Idaho Air National Guard back home.)

We learned that Chinook helicopters had dropped off the team in a canyon near the village, but as soon as they disembarked, hundreds of Taliban fighters ambushed them.

For the next thirteen hours, our troops returned fire. The TACPs on the ground called in air support from 14 different coalition aircraft, and I was piloting one of several MC-12s that provided high-tech "eye-in-the-sky" support during the fight. Even though there were hundreds of Taliban, they were well hidden in the rugged terrain and difficult to identify.

The radios were full of intense communications as we worked to ensure that the right munitions were being dropped in the right locations. It was truly a miracle that the combined efforts of everyone resulted in the death of 200 Taliban fighters—while not one American was injured. (The citation for my fourth oak leaf cluster on my air medal listed at the end of the book divulges more details about the battle.)

Several days after that intense firefight, the Air Force TACP who was on the ground during the battle showed up at our squadron. He had come to say "thank you" to the pilots who helped him survive. His wife had written thank you letters that included pictures of his family. He was extremely thankful to be alive, and he was grateful for the help our team had provided.

The Air Force awarded him a Silver Star, our country's third-highest award for combat valor for his heroic actions that day. I was honored to attend the ceremony at Joint Base Lewis-McChord in Washington, where he was presented with the Silver Star. There wasn't a dry eye in the room when he recounted his story of courage and faith. His bravery and humility exemplify the character and actions of a true American hero. I had the opportunity to serve with him again after we had both returned home from Afghanistan, and it was a poignant honor to meet his family. I was touched even further to find out that he had named his son "Ronin," after the warrior.

Curiously Strong

## *Chapter 21*

## *Chinook Down*

Those who are called to the profession of arms often hesitate to share stories from their battlefield experiences; most see it as a call to serve, not an opportunity for glory. I posted a military picture online and quickly had a fellow Airman chastise me for gloating. I believe there is a distinct difference between seeking personal glory and sharing accomplishments for other Americans to see—patriotism is something that can be lost if it is not carefully fostered.

It is for this reason that I carefully describe my deployment experiences; I would rather not share all the accounts, but I do want people to know what our service men and women do and realize that they keep doing it over and over daily. That is often overlooked by many media sources, most of which seem to want only to publicize mistakes the military makes, rather than the quiet heroism of so many of our service members.

Many of my friends and colleagues have both endured and accomplished far more than I have. Some have received less recognition, but still worked as diligent servants in the background, ensuring that radios were working, that the remains of our fallen comrades were properly honored, or thousands of other critical tasks that no one ever hears about are accomplished flawlessly. Two other deployment experiences are most memorable to me - one of pride and one of sorrow, both filled with the heroic acts of patriots.

My MC-12 squadron, the 4th Expeditionary Reconnaissance Squadron, set records for the number of flights we conducted. Troops on the ground always wanted eyes-in-the-sky above them, and there were a lot of troops to cover in Afghanistan. Flying operations in a warzone are intentionally sporadic. One of the tenets of combat operations is to avoid setting patterns, and between that and the high operations tempo our squadron had planes taking off at all hours of the day and night.

On May 2, 2011, I got up early enough to eat at the deployed dining facility during the midnight meal and got to work in time to brief up for my 2:00 a.m. mission and take off. I had been flying fairly regularly and had become somewhat inured to the routine of preparing for each sortie. Our aircraft were all parked in the same places on the flight line every day; there were MC-12s lined up as far as you could see and a few special operations aircraft periodically filling the distant parking spots.

I enjoyed flying in the early morning. It was the coolest part of the day in the hot desert, so my flight suit didn't get drenched in sweat during my walk to work. The air is also smoother in the morning, which makes flying quieter and less turbulent. There was always less air traffic to de-conflict with early in the morning, which made our navigation procedures simpler. May 2nd was just another day flying out of the largest Air Base in Afghanistan—until we all noticed something unusual.

We had just cranked up both engines and started inputting mission-related data when two special operations CV-22 Ospreys taxied right in front of us. Up to that point in my deployment, I hadn't seen Ospreys at Bagram—they are primarily a Navy asset. We carried out our mission, never giving it much more thought until we heard the news the next morning. A Navy SEAL team had killed Osama bin Laden during a raid in Pakistan.

I was never privy to information regarding the attack other than what was shared with the media. Based on what I saw, I'd like to guess that those Ospreys that taxied past us that morning took bin Laden's body out to sea. The capabilities of our armed forces are unfathomable, another one of the hundreds of reasons I'm proud to be an American.

The flying memory that lingers with me the most frequently was the day I experienced great sorrow. Members of the military make special commitments in their service for others, including putting their lives on the line for ideals bigger than themselves. One of the sobering truths about using God-given talents to serve is that some heroes give everything in their service to others.

In the final hours of August 5, 2011 two Chinook helicopters departed for a special operations mission in the Tangi Valley 60 miles southwest of Kabul. They successfully landed at their destination and debarked a group of Army Rangers who were tracking a senior Taliban leader. The Chinooks had already returned to home base when the Taliban fighters engaged our Rangers. Fighting forced the Taliban to split up into two groups, and SEAL Team Six was tasked with apprehending the second group.

The two Chinook helicopters departed the base again, this time with SEAL Team Six onboard, to return to the new location of the Taliban fighters; the first helicopter headed for the new landing zone with 38 US and allied service members and support personnel aboard. Unbeknownst to the aircrew, Taliban fighters had climbed up to an open-air roof; they shot multiple rocket-propelled grenades directly at the helicopter. Their second shot successfully hit the helicopter. All 38 personnel aboard were killed, making it the worst Fallen Angel event since World War II.

It took days for the ground personnel to secure the area and recover all the remains. During that time MC-12s provided continuous coverage from above. Under my lead, our MC-12 crew provided a combined total of 12 hours of over-watch for friendly forces during assault operations aimed at finding and prosecuting enemies in the area. Words can't describe the feelings that ran through me as I recounted talking to many of those same fallen SEALS on the radio just days before that tragic event. Those were some of the worst hours I have ever spent at the controls of an airplane.

To honor their service, the entire wing at Bagram, including most of the remaining SEALs, formed up on the flight line for a Fallen Angel memorial ceremony. We all watched in silence as each of the SEAL's flag-draped coffins were loaded into the back of a C-17 to be flown home honorably. Then each one of us filed behind the back of the plane to offer one last salute to those brave men, and I distinctly remember looking up and seeing one larger American flag that bannered over all their coffins. As that one flag took the shape of an angel and protected them on their flight home, I couldn't help but remember what those stars and stripes really stand for: the red for valor; the white for innocence; and the blue for vigilance, perseverance, and justice. There is no greater feeling of awe and humility, and ultimately, respect, than to watch another man give up his life for his commitment to freedom. Countless families were forever changed that day in the name of liberty.

Curiously Strong

# Chapter 22

## Single Engine Fears

The ejection process is quite extraordinary and should not be taken lightly. Pulling up on the ejection handles initiates a rapid, sequential process that completely disconnects the seat from the aircraft and launches it clear. Recent technology allows most ejection seats to be "zero, zero" which means that a pilot could be sitting stationary (at zero knots and zero altitude above ground) on the runway, pull the ejection seat handles and *probably* survive being violently removed from the emergency situation. There are many pilots who have lived through the ejection sequence, but most of them might tell you that ejecting is not as great a choice as it might sound.

The ejection process is really hard on the human body. Among other things, the enormous and near-instantaneous gravitational, or G-forces, exerted on the body compress the spine drastically during ejection. Research has indicated the human body can bear the stress of only two or three ejections, so it is for good reason that some pilots who have endured an ejection don't get the opportunity to fly in an ejection-seat aircraft again.

The second option, if a single-engine pilot has an engine failure, is to perform an engine-out, or "flame-out" landing. A flame-out landing in an F-16 is not as easy as it sounds. Therefore, pilots spend hours training and becoming experts on how to land their jet without an operating engine. They might argue that it is quite simple—once you get the hang of it.

Multi-engine fighter pilots would argue that flying a plane with more than one engine is the superior choice, but Air

Force pilots never intentionally fly with a failed engine. Even twin-engine planes have limitations—normally, the aircraft has a single-engine service ceiling, meaning it can only climb to and maintain a certain altitude when it's operating on only one engine. The other challenge is that many on-board aircraft systems are not redundant; they operate off a particular engine, and if that engine stops working, some of the aircraft's systems may shut down. Thankfully, aircraft engineers have split the systems when possible so that necessary systems continue to function to allow for a safe landing, regardless of which engine malfunctions.

Practicing what actions must be taken during an engine failure scenario is one of the most important emergency procedures that Air Force pilots train for. We practice engine failure situations monthly, if not weekly. We memorize emergency procedures for it, we talk about it, we practice on the ground, and we watch movies about other people who have experienced engine failure situations. I am very thankful to have always flown airplanes with two engines in combat.

On one particular day, I had the opportunity to put all those hours of practice to good use. The sun was starting to set on the evening of October 11, 2012 in the Khost Bowl, a valley 150 miles southeast of the capital city of Kabul in Afghanistan. Our MC-12 crew had been working with special operation forces from an Allied country to find a Taliban official in the area. The Khost Bowl is a relatively large, populated area that contains the thoroughfare to and from Pakistan and is surrounded by mountainous terrain with 16,000-foot peaks. We had been flying in the area for a little while when I noticed that something was wrong with the airplane.

It is standard operating procedure for pilots to periodically check the aircraft systems. Some pilots cross-check engine and other system indicators every fifteen to thirty minutes, depending on the duration of the flight. However, most pilots develop a more frequent cross-check of the status of their aircraft systems. I happened to be adjusting the throttle settings when I noticed the oil pressure indication on the left engine was decreasing. It continued to decrease outside of normal operating limitations. Instantly, my training regarding how to handle an impending engine failure kicked in, and I began a climb in altitude while simultaneously turning the aircraft back toward the base.

The emergency checklist requires the pilot to manually shut down the engine if the oil pressure decreases below 60 psi. The first priority was to reach an altitude that would allow us to clear the mountain range standing between us and our home base. With the oil pressure continuing to fall, I dedicated the entire last few minutes of power from the failing engine toward our climb to a safe altitude.

The second challenge after climbing to a safe altitude was to ensure the aircraft would be able to maintain that altitude above the 16,000-foot mountainous terrain while on power from only one engine. The next challenge was to quickly develop a plan to return to base with only half of the aircraft systems operable. I didn't want to shut down that failing engine until we could assure a safe landing on single-engine power.

It was a tense time, but all four of us remained calm and focused on our objective. We used our final moments of systems operations to handoff our tactical mission to the operators on the ground, and then quickly accomplished the emergency procedures checklist. We completed the required steps just before I had to manually shut down the engine to prevent a catastrophic failure. As the left propeller slowly came to a stop, we all gazed out the window in quiet amazement. It was a surreal image; the sun was setting behind a motionless propeller as we flew through the air above the mountains of Afghanistan. I prayed a silent prayer that we would get back to the base safely.

Thankfully, good training, a great crew, and efficient resource management ensured our safe flight back to the base. After landing, maintenance personnel informed us that an oil seal had ruptured. Our maintenance crews were top-notch, and the MC-12 engines are very durable, but all our aircraft were pushed to their limits while operating in the harsh Afghanistan environment.

## Chapter 23

## *Second and Third Trip to the Sandbox*

After my first tour in Afghanistan I was reassigned to Beale Air Force Base in Sacramento. This was the location for two new MC-12 squadrons after the Air Force transferred the MC-12 training operations from the Air National Guard to active-duty Air Force.

Upon my arrival at Beale I was tasked as chief of flight scheduling. Not long after that I also became a flight commander, with approximately 30 officers and enlisted personnel reporting to me. This is a standard progression for an Air Force pilot, and it gave me good additional leadership experience. I enjoyed living in central California where it was easy to keep up my workout regimen, and I had just finished my master's degree in exercise physiology and passed my test to be a certified personal trainer.

That summer I signed up for the Beale Air Force Base Fitness Championship and won another prize; this time for being the base's top female bench presser (it was a t-shirt, of course). After a few months of duty at the new base, I had an opportunity to return to Afghanistan. Since my desire had always been to serve our people fighting on the ground, it wasn't long before I was on a C-17 again, flying back to the Middle East.

The base where I was stationed had 35,000 people, but only half of those were from America. The rest were service members from other countries, foreign national staff, and locals from Afghanistan. It was mostly Afghan nationals who were cooking our food and doing other basic work. They also cleaned the gym, so I was able to interact with some of them fairly regularly. They had so much hope and thankfulness for what we were doing, which reminded me constantly of the blessings we Americans often take for granted. Some of them would ride a bus for hours to get to the base just to be a part of the fight for freedom.

The Afghanistan people I met were quite petite, so those assigned to cleaning the gym found it fascinating to watch me work out. Apparently, they were not used to seeing a tall woman, particularly one who could lift so much weight. One of the men told me he had a little girl, and I always encouraged him to help her be strong. Whenever I saw him I would ask him how she was doing. The base held a powerlifting competition in that gym and I signed up for old-time's sake. I trained for a few weeks leading up the competition and was surprised to take second place and received an award for being the "Strongest in the Area-Of-Responsibility" runner-up. The Afghani man was so impressed with my victory that he told his daughter about the competition.

This man's daughter was also the recipient of a special gift, even though I never got a chance to meet her. For Easter the base put on a nice dinner for us and they brought in some candy eggs and little stuffed toy bunnies to make it special. Thinking of this man's daughter, I arranged with the dining facility to get one of those bunnies along with a few pieces of candy. I made sure it was okay for an American female to give a Muslim man a gift, and I had to write a special note authorizing him to take the gift off the base. He was very touched when I told him to give it to his daughter to remind her to have hope and grow up strong.

Living on our base had its challenges. For example, we couldn't take showers longer than three minutes, all our trash had to be burned, and there was no local potable water. All our drinking water was bottled in Kabul and brought to the base.

Of all the roads on the base, only one of them was paved, and then only partially. That road's name was "Disney." Having something familiar from back home that we could all relate to helped with morale—we didn't feel quite so far away from home when asking someone to meet at the dining facility at the north end of Disney.

Flying missions came with the usual set of dangers, but even being on the base wasn't necessarily safe. The base was occasionally attacked by indirect fire, and it was almost always attacked on American holidays.

After my second deployment to Afghanistan I headed back to Beale Air Force Base, and just a couple months later we received some horrible news—an MC-12 had crashed in Afghanistan killing all four crewmembers. The news hit everyone in the MC-12 community hard. It was a sobering reminder of the dangers and tragedies of war, but I was anxious to get back in the fight, so I volunteered for a third Middle-East deployment. On this third trip I would not be flying. I would be planning, organizing, and coordinating flights at the Air Operations Center (AOC) in the Middle East. It was a good diversification for building my leadership abilities, as AOCs are much more strategically focused than tactical.

AOCs are the Air Force's main hubs for coordinating everything that happens in the air. Within AOCs, all the battle region's flights are scheduled, coordinated, monitored, and deconflicted. We also created backup plans for use in the event of contingencies. AOCs are where strategic decisions and priorities are weighed—nuts and bolts, gameplans, paperwork, and Air Tasking Orders run through the AOC. Before planes takes off, personnel at the AOC must know where it's going, why, where it's going to refuel—everything. All of this must be coordinated and then approved through the chain of command before a plane can take off.

In addition to tracking all manned flights, personnel at the AOC were also responsible for tracking all "drones," or unmanned aircraft, and for managing the flow of intelligence information. We accomplished all this while working closely with our NATO partners to coordinate our strategic plans. It was about big-picture thinking, marrying daily air operations with the military's overarching strategic vision.

One day while working at the Air Operations Center in the Middle East, I remember sitting next to a NATO representative from another country. He asked me why we Americans are so proud of our flag. He said that in his country, people were proud to live there, but they didn't feel it necessary to fly their nation's flag. His question seemed odd to me. Growing up, my family enjoyed flying our flag at home on special occasions, and I was used to seeing it flying at schools and city halls, as well as in many people's yards. As I pondered his question, I realized that many Americans are proud of our flag because of the freedom that it represents and the history of our distinctive origin as a nation.

Another question he asked that caught my attention was why we didn't have a mandatory voting policy in America. In his country, every person had to either vote or pay a fine. I told him I was thankful for the freedom I had in America to choose whether or not I wanted to vote. These questions along with other nuances of culture I had witnessed in my travel around the world gave me a new awareness of the many ways freedom influences our American culture. We travel freely, change jobs, choose our spouses, read without censorship, choose if and when we want children, choose our lifestyles, and much, much more. I often wonder how many of us take it all for granted.

Curiously Strong

## Chapter 24

## *My Golden Ticket Home to Idaho*

The word home has a variety of meanings for different people. For our service men and women who have deployed overseas, home has both deeper and more every-day meaning than the symbolic house with a white picket fence. Home means warm water coming out of a shower faucet. Home means walking barefooted on clean, carpeted floors. Home means sidewalks where children ride a bicycle and community parks for recreation and dog walking. Home means having a thousand choices of things to buy for dinner at a grocery store. Home means the freedom from unforeseen rocket attacks or roadside bombs. Home is having a neighbor who would be happy to lend a cup of sugar. Home is having a loving family close by. Home is the place where everyone wants to return to especially after sacrificing those luxuries on a deployment.

On my way home from being deployed I had the honor of catching a ride on a C-17 Galaxy. The C-17 is the workhorse of the Air Force of the United States and the world. A C-17 can carry tanks and helicopters among other things. Many of my college friends and pilot training colleagues still fly the C-17 to this day. For my return flight back to America from being deployed, I boarded a huge C-17 along with 50 other service members and by coincidence, I happened to know one of the pilots.

After a long flight across the ocean, the pilot came down to the cargo area and asked me if I wanted to accompany him up to the flight deck. Absolutely! I had never been up to the C-17 flight deck, and I was amazed by the massive size of it. Three pilots easily fit on the flight deck, with extra space

> **I wish every American had the opportunity to experience the powerful feeling of returning home after months of witnessing oppression and evil—the feeling of being welcomed home to safety and freedom by the sight of the shining sea in the morning.**

available for other crewmembers to sleep during long missions. I had thoughts of envy for a split second. However, the memory that is still etched in my mind, even more impressive than the massive cargo bay and spacious flight deck, was the view.

The sun was chasing our tail as the entire coastline of North America slowly appeared on the horizon. I just sat there in pure awe of our country. It took more than an hour to approach the East Coast; it started as a dark reflection in the distance, and then a distinct coastline, vivid skyscrapers, and beaches gradually appeared. The view of America's coastline tugged at my heart with all its beauty, the depth of its history, and the ideals of its founders. America and all its greatness is why our men and women serve, and it is why we love coming home. I wish every American had the opportunity to experience the powerful feeling of returning home after months of witnessing oppression and evil—the feeling of being welcomed home to safety and freedom by the sight of the shining sea in the morning.

## A New Chapter

After finishing my third deployment I returned once again to Beale Air Force base, home of the MC-12s, but it wasn't long before we received some shocking news. The Commander-in-Chief had ordered yet another budgetary cut, and the MC-12 program was getting the ax. It was frustrating. We had 400 Airmen who had been taken out of flying other airframes, and now we were getting pulled out of the MC-12 program too.

The rumor mill was churning. One rumor was that all 400 of us would be reassigned to fly unmanned aerial vehicles or "drones." That meant sitting in a room at a computer screen with a keyboard and directing a drone in the sky. To me it was like playing a video game, and I didn't want to do that, but I still owed the Air Force three more years on my 10-year obligation.

The rumor mill also suggested that I had a one-in-a-billion chance of getting selected for a program called *Palace Chase*. This program gave Airmen the opportunity to get out of an active duty military commitment if we promised to go serve in a Guard or Reserve unit. The trick was to find a Guard or Reserve unit that had an opening, which was tough since a mass Air Force-wide exodus to the Guard and Reserve during the previous force reduction had already recently occurred.

As fate would have it, a few people I knew at the Idaho Air National Guard in Boise had recently asked me to fly up to brief them on what the MC-12 program had been doing overseas. I flew up and gave a briefing, and while I was in town I heard about a potential job opening. I was excited about the opportunity to get back home to Idaho.

There was an opening; the position was as an Air Liaison Officer (ALO), and I was a perfect fit. My new role as the Air Liaison Officer was to be the senior air advisor to the ground commander, responsible for all levels of planning, advocacy and support of combined ground and air efforts in a combat environment.

When flying an attack aircraft that must employ ordnance in congested areas where friendly forces are in close contact with enemy forces, or when civilians are nearby, it is critical to have someone on the ground in that location, or otherwise close-by, who is intimately aware of the ground battle situation, and who is in radio contact with attack pilots. This person, often embedded with ground troops, is trained in the critical Air Force role of a Joint Terminal Attack Controller (JTAC). Our Rules of Engagement mandated weapons employment be cleared when possible through JTACs. With their eyes on the target and trained to coordinate and communicate with both ground and air forces, they were able to pass incredibly accurate coordinates to aircrews for precision weapons impact and minimal collateral damage. An Air Liaison Officer is an experienced pilot who works with ground commanders as well as JTACs, helping them understand how to safely and effectively use crucial air support to accomplish their ground battle objectives.

I submitted my request for consideration to separate from the active duty Air Force under the Palace Chase program, and to my surprise, my seemingly one-in-a-billion chance to transition into the Reserve component of the Air Force was actually approved. On July 1, 2014, I became the first female Air Liaison Officer in the Idaho Air National Guard. The transition to Gowen Field was a career-broadening move into a position of increased leadership responsibilities. I was tasked with leading troops on the ground, as well as with sharing my experience from a pilot's point of view with ground troops so they could more effectively use available air power to their advantage when in combat.

As a "traditional" National Guardsman, I served one weekend a month, and two full weeks each year. Transitioning from full-time to part-time employment meant a cut in pay, so I needed other employment options. I needed a new direction. I began researching airline employment opportunities, and the process for obtaining my commercial airline pilot's license. I had gained plenty of valuable experience during my active duty career, but now the question was, "What do I do with it?" I still wanted to make a difference.

This practical career question hung in the air while I made the psychological transition from military to civilian life. I had some seriously deep thinking to do while I decompressed from the warrior lifestyle and transitioned to home and family life. Like most of the troops heading home after extended deployments overseas, I had to make sense of the world I had been living in.

## *Part Three: Curiously Strong Leadership*

**cu· ri· ous· ly** (3)

Adverb

1. in a strange, unusual or unexpected way.

**strong**

Adjective

1. morally powerful; able to think vigorously and clearly.
2. well established.

**lead· er· ship**

Noun

1. the activity of influencing through vision, motivation, serving, empathy, creativity, and team building to reach a common goal.
2. having the capacity to lead.
3. the office or position of a leader.

## *Chapter 25*

## *Emotional Maturing*

I bought a house; it was not a perfect house, but it was my house. While I was on active duty I would never have been able to buy a house—or at least the kind of house that needed someone to invest time and effort into restoring it. This house was an investment; I could see potential to turn a marginal, run down house into a respectable small home. The house was more than just a project though, it was what I needed to *do,* to work on, to change, to install floors and new counters— to find a new side of myself. When I transitioned to civilian life and moved back home to Idaho, I was looking forward to the adventure of finding a new "normal." I found that normal pace in restoring the house that needed me as much as I needed it.

The military lifestyle is demanding; it requires lots of moving, training in unique locations, travel, and sporadic work schedules. While I enjoyed the adventure, I sometimes experienced the lingering feeling that I was missing out on a "normal" life. I longed for a routine, predictable schedule in which I could join a club and commit to regular meetings—a schedule where I could actually find a nice church and not feel guilty about having to miss scheduled events.

As a woman, I also felt challenged by the daunting task of managing the delicate balance between work and family life. Dating and establishing a long-term relationship with someone had been nearly impossible, especially with periodic long deployments. I looked forward to the future opportunity of starting a family free from the stressors of military life.

Easing into my new "normal" life in Idaho, I finally had time to reflect on who I had become, and what my experiences had taught me. I knew the answers to my reflections would help guide my transition into a much-desired new routine; and that it would take time to process those old feelings I had pushed aside out of necessity, during my whirlwind of life experiences. Now, I wanted to consciously study and reflect on my experiences, so that I could apply their lessons in a positive way to my new life. It was the heavy lifting of wading through these emotions and memories that made me realize that returning home after three separate deployments proved to be far more psychologically challenging than actually living in a combat zone.

Living in a combat zone was actually quite simple; everyone learned to push his or her emotions to the back burner in order to focus on the mission. Avoidance was a key attribute that warriors bragged about. I recounted the dozens of times that male leaders remarked, "We can't afford to have you make mistakes due to personal problems, so compartmentalize your troubles, check them at the door before you come into work." That made sense to us.

Emotions do have an impact on your performance, sometimes enough to cause a life or death situation when you're flying high performance aircraft. Even though I took pride in being able to compartmentalize my emotions, or "check them at the door," I intrinsically knew that I couldn't keep it choked down forever.

But when I returned home from my deployments, I was still grappling with the effects of the injustices I had witnessed, the loss of friends who I watched die and my fellow pilots who didn't get to return home with me. Even though I had my own emotional scars to try to heal, I was still responsible for leading fellow Airmen who hadn't yet mastered the "curiously strong" coping skills I had developed. So I pushed my own emotional burdens aside to help them learn.

I saw young men and women shunned and careers destroyed, because they didn't know how to emotionally process the horrors of war they had witnessed and experienced first-hand. I listened to countless stories from colleagues whose wives left them. For many, alcohol became their only way of coping with indescribable emotions. I waded through the process of filling out Veterans Affairs (VA) paperwork for both myself and others, because many under my command had become so frustrated and resigned that they were unable to fight through the government red tape. We had to make do and figure the processes out ourselves, usually failing multiple times, and having to learn from one another's mistakes in order to successfully get through it. The majority of my friends and Airmen just threw away the paperwork in disgust.

Finally home, away from the military stressors that had been "checked at the door" emotionally, I allowed myself time for personal reflection. I had helped Airmen under my command deal with complicated personal situations and it then took me a considerable amount of time to search my own memories for the events in my life that had helped me cope up until this point. I had to teach myself how to rediscover those emotions, process them, and put them to work for me in a positive way.

## *Cry Baby Cry*

Growing up I hadn't liked it when my brothers called me a crybaby, so I learned how to turn off my tears. When I set my sights on becoming a military officer, I assumed that officers never cried, so I promised myself that I wouldn't either.

On in-processing day at the Air Force Academy, the abrupt shift from being a civilian to becoming a war-fighter hit me hard. Basic training was a vigorous program designed to turn high school students into Airmen and leaders, and I renewed my resolved to never cry, no matter how difficult it was. At that time, I shared the common emotional misconception that a responsible leader was always tough— inside and out.

When I arrived at the Academy for Basic Training "boot camp," I mistakenly received combat boots two sizes too large in the rush of getting uniforms issued. I thought it was not worth drawing attention to myself, so I kept quiet. After days of rigorous physical training, running, and practically sleeping in those boots, my feet were on fire, covered in blisters. Still not wanting to highlight myself, I tried to suck it up, but one evening during exercise drills, I wasn't getting my knees up high enough.

That caused the upperclassmen cadre overseeing our cadet training to center their attention on my lack of performance. One very large, mean guy marched over to me, and with his face within millimeters of my face demanded, "Why can't you hack it, Giddings?" At that moment, my eyes filled with the beginning of a tear, yet I managed to ensure no tears escaped to roll down my face. The tears welling in my eyes instantly set him off with more condescending remarks, "Are you crying already, Giddings?" The shear embarrassment of him alluding that I might cry reinforced my resolve to never, ever cry, or even so much as let my eyes get watery again—as if I could control it.

So, I never cried again, that is, until I started pilot training. Thankfully I had a wonderful roommate while I was going through pilot training, she was far wiser than I was about emotional health. Her dream was to be an aerial refueling pilot. Her fiancé was going to be a Navy fighter pilot and she wanted to fly a plane that would allow them to be stationed near one another. Her plan worked out perfectly; years later she and her husband made the national news when her aircraft refueled his fighter jet during combat operations overseas. They are an unstoppable couple that I admire and respect greatly, but the thing I appreciated the most about her as my roommate was that she taught me that it is okay to cry. It is foolish to think that crying can be separated from healthy human behavior; there are times when it is acceptable, and even necessary to cry.

My roommate and I were both working hard through the rigors of flight training in our separate programs. It seemed to me that she cried *a lot*, and I could not relate to that, at least at first. We all worked twelve-hour days and locked ourselves in our rooms on the weekends to catch up on studying. Even though we were roommates, we hardly saw one another. One day when I had gotten back from a really rough day, she walked in the door already in tears. The floodgates burst open!

We stood next to each other by the washer and dryer in the laundry room and unloaded months' worth of stress and hardships. We both cried rivers of tears, which eventually turned into laughter when we recognized how pitiful we looked. As we walked away from our only group cry session, we both resolved that we had worked too hard to stop now, and that we were going to get through the challenges that faced us. Having the freedom to navigate the emotional burdens with another strong female leader sure made me feel better. I was even stronger after that.

I am not sure I would have made it through everything I faced if I had continued along the "stuff-it-down" path. People certainly need some way to cope with extreme stress, and there is no reason to think that the coping mechanisms that work for men have to be equally effective for women, or to assume that the traditional, "approved" coping mechanisms are even working for our male troops.

Studies of the emotional health of predominately male troops returning from combat have confirmed alarmingly high rates of Post-Traumatic Stress Disorder, or PTSD, family violence, and divorce rates—all caused or exacerbated by long deployments and other unsung, service-related sacrifices. These problems are still poorly understood, and poorly dealt with. The military has well documented the high suicide rates of service men and women. I contend that the traditionally insensitive and often emotionless environment of the military is a contributing factor to mental health breakdowns within the military's ranks.

There is no doubt that the pressure can be terrible to bear, and we need to continue building and validating healthy and natural coping mechanisms, one of which, as I found out that day, is crying. I pray for the day that our military will acknowledge, understand and accept the expanded strength and benefit of full emotional awareness and balance.

For myself, learning how to cry was helpful during my emotional maturing process. I finally let myself react naturally to a stressor, rather than trying to stifle my reaction as expected by others. I find it liberating to be able to confidently rely on all my instinctual coping mechanisms, and I hope that one day, many of our returning veterans will find their own healthy ways to deal with their often tremendous levels of overwhelming stress. For me, my newfound self-assurance in emotional expression helped me become more fully myself.

# Curiously Strong

## Chapter 26

## *Bring Me Women*

I will never devalue the work of my commanding officers and colleagues. I feel great respect for everything our military leaders have accomplished. In fact, our military is often a step ahead of our society in regard to setting social standards and leading positive change. Our military has taken incredible strides toward welcoming women into its ranks and encouraging them to succeed in roles once closed off to women. Yet in many areas, there is still work to be done. While working in environments devoid of feminine influence or representation beyond my own, I often pondered the unique qualities and strengths females bring to the fight.

Let me start by making some broad thesis statements about my gender that I believe are generally accepted as true. Women nurture our future generations and predominately run our elementary schools (and yes, those would be better off with more men present). Women teach our Sunday school classes and run our volunteer organizations. They nurse people back to health, set the moral compass for children, encourage, listen, and aren't afraid to shed tears.

Women have a great capacity to analyze complex, multi-level situations with compassion and practical common sense. They possess a strong social conscience and find creative ways to stretch limited resources. They pay attention to the details. I could list much more, but the point is that women are already recognized for important contributions to our society.

Many of these innate female character traits are not carried up the ladder to the next level of leadership, policy making, and governance. In the past it has not been socially acceptable for women to get involved in leadership roles; this is changing, but often women try to play at being a man in a "man's world" rather than using their innate strengths in their leadership roles, and so the associated

> **Often women try to play at being a man in a "man's world" rather than using their innate strengths in their leadership roles.**

changes in society are lagging behind. Women who aspire to lead will likely need to teach their peers this new leadership paradigm, a leadership that envelopes and promotes both masculine and feminine leadership characteristics.

## It's Not Always a "Pissing Contest"

Perhaps one of the reasons women are more aptly skilled at identifying and fulfilling needs is that we aren't always on "high alert" since we aren't generally conditioned at a young age to perceive every situation as a competition—or as some of my male friends refer to it, a "pissing contest." Women can also be extremely competitive but are often able to adjust their personal reactions to meet the needs of the moment.

I witnessed many women trying to compete with men by following the rules of their intra-male hierarchy, and they nearly always lost. I knew of one female fighter pilot who made incredible attempts at "keeping up with the guys" through drinking, swearing, and dipping tobacco as much as they did—but it only hurt her performance in the long run.

In pilot training, I found I was too tired to play the "game" and I really didn't want to, so I just decided to be myself. Instead of bringing alcohol to the Friday night "mandatory fun" events, it seemed more my nature to bring homemade cookies. The plate was always emptied in seconds. My male colleagues did not perceive me as a threat. They often referred to me as a "sister." At those times they would banter playfully with me, but they usually didn't verbally insult me as often as they did the other men in their perpetual need to establish a pecking order.

However, there were times during pilot training when I was perceived as a threat because of my performance or gender, and I needed to perform at my highest level to maintain my seat in training. Even then, I wasn't focused on competition, but rather on doing my best to accomplish the task or challenge before me. I believe that more important than establishing dominance in a situation of limited resources and positions, human beings ought to strive for excellence, to give their all to the situation at hand, instead of worrying about externally influenced outcomes. Striving for personal excellence usually takes care of the results, and negates the need to run others over in the process. In fact, it is when we are doing our best that we become more selfless—more apt to truly see, and willing to meet, the needs of others.

## A Good Spotter

One observation I made about the female leaders in the military units where I served is that they tended to fill the role of helping fellow Airmen navigate personal issues. The female leaders were nearly always first to initially *notice* an Airman's needs, and it was with the female leaders that fellow Airmen felt comfortable talking about their uncomfortable or complex situations with. This seemed especially true in cases where there were no simple, direct answers to their problems.

Throughout my career, I came to realization that meeting the emotional needs of individuals makes the entire group stronger, but there were many barriers to an individual receiving appropriate counseling while serving in the Air Force. Seemingly endless amounts of red tape stopped people from asking for help before they ever made it in the door to talk to someone. Additionally, the stigma and potential career implications of receiving formalized counseling deterred many from seeking help. The important conversations were instead happening in back offices, and in the gym between sets. A physical spotter also served as an emotional spotter, by providing the necessary emotional support to persevere during tough situations.

I noticed that the female leaders seemed to be the ones with the most effective relationship-building skills, which enabled them to help others process the stresses of life, and to mend moral injuries. Officially, a military Chaplain fills these roles, yet many Airmen often don't feel their situations are serious enough to bother a chaplain, so they turn to friends, and usually seem more willing to open up to women. I often noticed it was the women who demonstrated compassionate, non-judgmental approach, without posing a threat to males' masculinity.

Perhaps this is why I seemed to perform so much better back in T-38 training when I was given the opportunity to fly with one of the three female instructors. It seemed like she allowed me to let my guard down, be a little vulnerable, and truly learn how to conquer new flying challenges. These reflections challenge me to recognize that women have a very valuable place as leaders in the niches of our society.

## Bitchin' Betty

An average A-10 costs over twenty million dollars, even more now with expensive avionics systems upgrades. Nearly every essential piece of information needed to employ weapons is projected onto a Heads-Up Display, or HUD, positioned between the pilot and the windscreen. Recently, helmet-mounted display technology has enabled the same aircraft and weapons data to be displayed on the pilot's visor. Even with all the cutting-edge visual technology, a few crucial warnings are still audio recordings.

If the pilot is heads-down looking inside the cockpit while flying and encounters a potentially lethal situation outside the jet, such as getting too close to the ground, or flying close to terrain, the computer system sends verbal cues to the headset in a *female* voice. The cues loudly repeat things like "Pull up, pull up" or "Eject, eject." The pilot term for this voice is "Bitchin' Betty" and in the A-10 it is *always* a female voice. Instructors in my training course explained that it was specifically designed to be a female voice after behavioral engineers discovered that men reacted more quickly to a female voice in high stress situations.

When I was training to become a pilot, we were graded on communication every day. My male instructors made it a point to always tell the women to lower the octave of their voices on the radio; they told us it made us sound more professional and others would more effectively listen to us better if we used a lower octave. I spent those months and years trying to lower the tone of my voice well enough to receive good communication scores, and when I finally finished my training, I sounded more like Darth Vader on the radio.

I learned a lot more about communication once I deployed overseas and started talking on the radio frequently. I would be flying over remote parts of Afghanistan, checking in with troops on the ground. Some of the men I spoke with (Navy SEALS, Rangers, and other Special Operations guys) had been out in the desert for weeks or months without interacting with women. When I checked in on the radio, I chuckled at how many of those guys on the ground wanted to hear me talk. I would even get requests at the base specifically asking for me to run a mission so they could hear a female voice, and they did NOT want to hear my Darth Vader voice.

We also responded to several intense troops-in-contact situations. As a pilot with a clear picture of the ground from my vantage point, it was imperative that I maintained a calm voice no matter how tense the situation was. Those experiences made me reassess the value of the female voice. There are appropriate times to change octaves, and in fact voice control can have significant impact on the outcome of certain situations. The point that those instructors in pilot training missed by fixating on our female voices was that a lot of additional information can be transmitted by voice tone, pitch, inflection, and cadence, whether intentional or not.

Emergency dispatchers work with this reality every day, and it is eminently valuable for women to develop an understanding of their vocal skills and then learn how to adjust them to maximize professional gain. This significance is also why it is imperative that women leaders chose their words wisely. As women, we hold a lot of power with our voices, and carefully chosen tone and words can often greatly influence a situation's outcome. There are many variables, but a few I have especially noticed are; the calm, confidant tone that reassures the listener, a shrill, whiney voice that can be irritating, and a shaky or rising tone that can transfer nervousness.

Aside from tone, a large portion of communication occurs through body language, and women often seem to be first to notice changes in body language. We all know it is the women in our lives who first notice our sadness or emotional changes. In politics, using physical indicators to assess a situation provides a stiff advantage over male politicians (one of the many reasons I believe women make better government spokesmen, and a reason I hope we continue to fill political positions across the country and world).

## *Hear What I See*

Women tend to incorporate tone and body language into building shared mental models, giving them a communication advantage. During A-10 training, I struggled to keep up with the guys on memorizing mechanics and systems information, and it *seemed* like I always ended up last in the class when it came to systems knowledge. The only day that I won an academic training exercise consisted of a timed verbal test in which the testee had to verbally instruct a blindfolded partner how to draw a diagram. I was by far the fastest student to provide the verbal cues necessary for the blindfolded pilot to draw the required diagram, and it was no coincidence.

Creating a shared mental model is an important skill for fighter pilots. They often have to communicate with other pilots or troops on the ground who don't have the same bird's eye view with a process referred to as a "talk on." When a pilot identifies a target on the ground she or he has to verbally guide the other pilot's eyes to see the same target by providing information in a big to small sequence: "Do you see the river?" "Do you see the L-shaped road on the north side of the river?" "Do you see the red-roofed building next to the L-shaped road?" and then "Do you see the armored tank parked next to the L-shaped building?" I have found that this same "talk on" technique works in construction, law enforcement, and even politics. Building shared mental models is part of a verbal intelligence trait where female leaders often seem to have a natural advantage.

Some might argue that the ability to construct shared mental models falls within the scope of personality difference, not gender. If my personality were more communicative naturally, I might agree, but I've generally found that it is easier for women to verbally communicate these large concepts. It follows naturally that female leaders can pick up on body language cues if one understands the issue and thus interprets the message accurately. This is a huge advantage for leaders who must often make judgments on the fly.

## Silly Pink Perspectives

In the military it seems that the shared mental model for a tough Airman is one that is strong, composed, stoic. This image comes from a history of male leadership. In fact, there was a study done in 1954 by Raymond Cattell who concluded that top military leadership traits consisted of emotional stability, dominance, enthusiasm, conscientiousness, social boldness, tough-mindedness, self-assurance, and compulsiveness.

None of these qualities fit the common perception of femininity, but it is an image military women often strive to fulfill anyway. This image is why my upperclassmen mocked me for that unreleased tear that involuntarily welled in my eye. Historically men have often been repulsed by the idea of women serving in the military because women are different, because their expectation of women is to be the opposite of men: soft and fuzzy, pretty and pink.

It is not just men who have cultural baggage about femininity. Cultural norms are present in the silliest most pervasive ways. I never wanted to be a cheerleader; I couldn't relate to anyone who did. I was big, strong, and quiet—the antithesis of a cheerleader. I hated pink just because so many people assumed that all girls like pink.

I developed these attitudes early on in my childhood, and I started to resent anyone who assumed that my favorite color was pink or that I wanted to play with dolls and be a cheerleader in school. I remember feeling pressured to want to be a cheerleader; but I wasn't built to be a cheerleader, I was built to be a powerlifter. So I secretly snubbed cheerleaders because I couldn't relate with them, and I consciously avoided pink.

When I became a fighter pilot, I instantly developed a new love for pink. Male fighter pilots hated pink—they didn't just hate it, they would not even say the word pink. I'm really not sure of the reasoning behind some fighter pilot traditions, and don't want to know. When all the pink highlighters got thrown away at work, I valued the free markers more than my image and I started using more pink highlighters.

That's when it dawned on me that these little modified behaviors were masculinity tests that I didn't have to compete with. Because I was a woman, I was allowed to use the pink markers. Then I started using everything that was pink, because I didn't have to worry about it getting "misplaced" when no one in the squadron would touch it. Pink earplugs, pink clip board, pink folders, no matter what it was, I didn't have to put my name on it. Everyone knew that the pink one was mine.

My juvenile disliking of cheerleaders and the color pink came back full circle to underscore the hidden aspects of female leadership as my military experiences made me recognize the healthy need for cheerleaders and feminine (pink) perspectives. While I was serving alongside some incredible women in Afghanistan, I discovered that everyone needs a cheerleader once in a while to encourage them through tough times. My cheerleader friends in Afghanistan just happened to wear camouflage.

## *Chapter 27*

## *Cheerleaders in Combat Boots*

As I've mentioned a few times before, most of my Air Force career I have been in the minority, if not the only female. It was isolating and lonely, but it refined in me an inner confidence in the value of my own feminine strength. I brought something different to the table than my male counterparts, and I learned that this was a good thing. It is great that women do things differently than men, because women *are* different from men.

Women cannot easily pee at 25,000 feet and at 300 miles per hour, and most men don't relieve their stress and tension by crying or snacking. These differences are all ok; what is not okay is that often women feel they cannot excel in a male dominated environment because of their femininity. Women should leverage their femininity by using those skills intrinsic to their nature to succeed, while still respecting the masculine manifestations of their male counterparts' leadership.

It is difficult to do this without the support of other women; we tend to flock together just to go to the restroom, and the "lonely at the top" leadership style doesn't always fit our natural tendencies. With this in mind, it becomes apparent that it is much more important for us to have each other's support while facing all of life's challenges. This is also where we can put our natural talents to work: as encouragers.

## *Encouragers*

Women leaders are natural encouragers, and I feel strongly that we should encourage excellence rather than basic performance. Just as a "negative" lift overwhelms the muscles to stimulate faster growth, so encouragement calls out what is unseen into reality. It is important for our society that leaders rediscover true encouragement, the calling forth of true potential, NOT sweet words to sugar coat feelings of inadequacy. True encouragement is rather like the "good, but I know you can do more" response from someone who cares which inspires personal motivation to meet higher standards. In other words, true encouragement is a "negative" (lift)!

Women leaders can have huge impact on the success of those in their spheres of influence by using encouragement. Although it is helpful for both men and women, encouragement from women leaders is particularly helpful to other women. This is especially true when those women have

> **It is important for our society that leaders rediscover true encouragement, the calling forth of true potential, NOT sweet words to sugar coat feelings of inadequacy.**

become mired in the minutia of the day-to-day struggle of getting a job done. Because females think and process events on multiple levels, their mental and emotional thought processes can also lead to the trap of over-thinking their situations. This is often where timely encouragement can be enormously helpful.

## You'll Get Through This!

There is a tradition of completing a recognition course at the end of the freshman year at the Academy. This marks the end of a cadet's Doolie year when they become an upper-class cadet. There are forty days of grueling tasks leading up to the final recognition day, for which every Doolie lives in great anticipation. The recognition course marks the end of being treated like a freshman, and the beginning of a somewhat more normalized college experience.

The other significant tradition of recognition occurred after we completed all the grueling challenges, when we went through a special ceremony to receive our very own *prop and wings*. The prop and wings pin was then attached to our hats and served as a symbol to the entire cadet wing that we had been accepted as upperclassman. Some cadets' family members, who also graduated from the Academy or earned their prop and wings in one of several other ways, saved theirs to pass down as tokens of accomplishment within the family line.

For me, anticipation of the recognition week activities included the secret hope that I could just endure the endless push-ups. I didn't have any family members to pass me their prop and wings, but something unique happened that made me feel just as special and motivated me to get through the rigorous recognition events—one of my track teammates who was an upperclassman came over to my squadron and found me when no one else was looking. She preemptively gave me a special set of prop and wings with a few choice words, "When times get tough, just remember that it will all be worth it in the end. I'm confident that you'll get through this."

The fact that she took time to provide *me* with some individual encouragement motivated me to endure the tough exercises. To this day I reflect on how important it has been in my life when women I looked up to took the time to provide me with some individual, personalized words of encouragement. It always made a great improvement to my confidence, moral, and mental stamina; those gifts of personal encouragement served as beacons lighting my way through tough challenges.

**It is this authentic sensitivity that makes a woman leader irreplaceable.**

I also found that during times in my career when I had role models I knew personally, they led me more effectively to successes. Having another woman a step ahead of me, or one who had already achieved a goal I was working toward, motivated me to keep going. It was during times when I was isolated from other women, role models, and their encouragement that I was most likely to struggle to progress toward achieving my goals.

Strong female leaders recognize the importance of these encouragement encounters and use them to support the people around them in their lives. As humans, we all learn from others' experiences, and it is very important to share the lessons we learn in life with others.

It is during the raw moments when we admit those things that worked or didn't work, that we open up new ideas and opportunities for those following in our footsteps. It is this authentic sensitivity that makes a woman leader irreplaceable.

I read a recent study about the success of children that was highlighted in Dr. Angela Duckworth's book, *Grit: The Power of Passion and Perseverance*. Researchers found that children who were constantly reassured about their performance gave up easily after encountering very difficult problems, but children who were continually encouraged to do just a little better tried harder after encountering difficulty. Mantras like "You are capable of more" trigger patterns of excellence far more than phrases like "you did a good job."

I have heard considerable discussion in recent years about the idea of giving every child a trophy to encourage participation and help them feel good about their accomplishments. I feel that practice sends messages of low expectation: "You're doing fine." "You can be satisfied with what you have already done." I would not find these messages encouraging or motivational, and according to the study cited in *Grit* it actually does have an opposite effect and that can limit achievement.

I think back to the female pilots who pulled us future officers aside at the Air Force Academy years ago to offer us some individualized, intentional mentoring. I appreciated them for it then, but even more so now that I realize how lasting an effect that simple effort had. They noticed there was a need, took the initiative to communicate, encouraged, and left a legacy of strong female leaders behind them. They essentially told us that the road ahead was going to be difficult, but "hang in there, we did it—and you can too." I am determined to follow their model of mentoring and encouraging other women by continuing to put to good use those female leadership traits that they used to help us.

## The Legacy of Rosie the Riveter

Right after the Japanese attacked Pearl Harbor during World War II there was a shortage of military pilots. There was a huge need that couldn't be filled quickly enough. That is when hard-working American women stepped up to fill the

> **I firmly believe that being a strong female leader does not include insulting or belittling the value of men in our world.**

need. Between 1942 and 1944 more than a thousand women were trained to fly, and they eventually became known as the Women Airforce Service Pilots (WASPs). They ended up flying every aircraft in the Army and filled aviation roles at 120 bases across the country.

I had the honor of meeting a WASP, Betty Wall Strohfus, before she passed away in 2016. Her personality was as big as her history. My favorite memory from meeting her was when she said, "Well I tell ya girls, if you want to do something, do it! As long as it isn't illegal or immoral, then go for it!"

Just as the WASPs filled a need during World War II, today women leaders are able to identify and fill leadership needs; it just requires a little adaptability and creativity. Strong intelligent women must recognize the value of men in society and their strengths within the group. The same is true of the need for intelligent male leaders to value female characteristics. I firmly believe that being a strong female leader does not include insulting or belittling the value of men in our world as is trendy in some circles. My respect and admiration for men, especially American men, continues to grow.

Even so, as I struggled through my years of pilot training, the moments when I was validated in my femininity uplifted and inspired me, and I know that there are women who need to be validated in their femininity by the men in their lives, as my father did for me. I wouldn't be where I am today, would not have contributed to our war effort, nor been there to help save lives, if my family had been content to limit me by past societal gender roles. But that was not their perspective; my family's "can do" attitude pushed me to succeed with my God-given strengths whatever they were and never placed gender-biased expectations on me.

This matters because I perceive that there is still a "gender-gap" in leadership today. Some of the necessary changes have already occurred, but it takes time for the women to "trickle up" into leadership positions. There does not have to be an uprising or social protest to demand female leadership. There isn't a quota we need to fill with women leaders, we just need enough that no one finds it unusual when a woman steps up to take on the role, and that aspiring women leaders have other women to teach them. Women, I say to you, just do it. You don't need permission.

Curiously Strong

## Chapter 28

## *Transitioning from Combat to the State Capitol*

In November of 2016, I was elected to serve in the Idaho State House of Representatives. It did not take long to see the need for someone who could apply skilled leadership like strategic planning, organization, reliable principles of ethics, and effective communication. Too many of the people who were serving "on the ground" back home in state government were not committed to those they represented. The purpose and goals of the state's business seemed to be muddled and disconnected from the will of the people. The process was broken. I was disappointed that so many thought this was normal.

My path to the State Capitol was a natural progression of events, which first began early in high school. My sophomore year I was a young volunteer at a US Senator's regional office and the next year I served as a page at the state legislature in Boise, so I became somewhat familiar with political atmosphere. At that time, I was not particularly interested in being a politician, but I thought the volunteer work was interesting.

Years later when I left active military service and transitioned to the Air Guard and then eventually the Reserves, I talked with my local state senator about helping out in her office. I knew that it was a busy job and I was interested in helping where I could. The state senator knew my family and offered me a volunteer position as her aide during the upcoming legislative session.

Idaho is one of many states that have a part-time legislature; it meets for only three months out of the year. Due to limited funding for legislative staff, a legislator can take on a college intern, if one is available, or they must complete their staff work themselves. I knew of another female fighter pilot who was working as a legislative aide in California, and I was interested to learn about state politics, so I agreed to volunteer as my senator's aide in my spare time during the three-month session. This was an opportunity for me to be proactively involved in something that was very important to me—the cause of freedom in Idaho.

## Free People

I had observed several different forms of government as I traveled widely during my active duty years, and it was surprisingly clear to see the grass-roots impact of each form of government on their people. I have traveled to more than 30 nations around the world and there were only a handful of countries that came close to providing the comforts and advantages we enjoy in America. Some of the worst examples I witnessed were in the Middle East and Africa.

I spent nearly 1,000 hours in the skies over Afghanistan, and during those deployments I saw people everywhere living in fear of the Taliban. The Afghan people weren't allowed to practice religious freedom. Women feared being injured or killed because they were women, and they weren't allowed to work, drive, or travel alone. Fear ruled over everyone, and there was no rule of law to secure individual rights, only capricious Taliban laws. The people were at their mercy.

One of the objectives of America's counter-insurgency operations was to change the way people in Afghanistan did things. We brought them a legal process, and we attempted to assist them in using that process, because they didn't have the structure or foundation of a constitution espousing basic principles of good government.

During my time overseas, I also remember calling home and talking with my dad. I recall him telling me that policies were being implemented in Idaho without our state legislature voting on them and describing the resulting grief it caused with individuals and businesses. I thought, "How can this be?" I feared this meant we were slowly beginning to lose our grasp on our freedoms, and that our form of representative government might be at risk. I recall thinking that our legislators should be voting on matters that support our citizens, not letting government agencies impose their policies on the citizens.

> **You can taste how valuable freedom is when you're watching the extreme opposite of it.**

This is one of the reasons why I agreed to be an aide in my state legislature. You can taste how valuable freedom is when you're watching the extreme opposite of it. People were starving for freedom in Afghanistan, while in Idaho it seemed like those freedoms were silently slipping away while no one was looking.

In Afghanistan, we were trying to foster the idea of freedom and teach people how to fight for it. I confidently believed that I could use the leadership skills I had acquired in the Air Force and join the struggle to retain freedom at home. I could sense the gradual slipping from my vantage point, but I wasn't sure how pervasive or serious it might be. I was confident that no one in their right mind would want to abandon our representative republic, and I didn't see any major changes that were needed. But I have seen, up close and personal, the end result of societies who have no power or personal freedoms all around me while overseas. So, I had to get involved.

I used my time as an aide to help the senator serve her constituents in whatever ways I could, usually by helping them navigate the red tape of state or federal agencies. During one of those efforts, I needed to contact the office of one of Idaho's US Senators. We needed his help to resolve a federal restriction placed on one of my state senator's constituents, and I worked as the liaison to get that issue resolved. I found I enjoyed the kind of work that enabled me to make a difference, even when it was for just one person at a time. The troops in this field (the citizens) needed a strong defender.

By the summer of 2015, the legislative session ended, and I had learned a lot about complex political gears. Politics was calling to me, but I needed to earn a real paycheck relatively soon. I resumed my preparation to apply for an airline pilot job by completing the requirements for my Airline Transport Pilot certificate. Then one day, I was surprised with a call from the same Idaho US Senator's office, offering me a job. His office was gearing up for the Senator's re-election campaign, and they asked me to serve as a campaign field director.

A choice was laid out before me. I had already identified a commercial airline I was interested in working for, and was getting things ready to fly for them, but now I had a new political opportunity to consider. I knew it would be a temporary opportunity, because US Senate elections occur only every six years. I decided to accept and delayed my airline career prospects once more.

Being a campaign field director meant a lot of traveling, attending community events, public speaking, and meeting a lot of people. I filled this role for eight months, meeting with Idahoans and campaigning for the senator. Along the way, I realized that I enjoyed speaking to groups about issues and interacting with the public. I poured over current issues and plowed through a pile of reading, connected with mentors, and familiarized myself with the political network. I thought that if I ever decided to run for public office, it would be satisfying work.

I also became more acquainted with the current state representative in my district. Although she had a very conservative voting record, she had some health concerns and was having a difficult time being a strong voice for the district. I respected her and had even voted for her. But, after long consideration, I knew I could be a stronger voice for freedom and liberty, and that I could make a stand for rural values in Idaho, which I felt—and still do—was desperately needed.

The first week of March 2016, I decided to run for office to represent Idaho's very large District 7. The primary was only two months away, and I campaigned hard. My efforts gained me a 61% victory over the incumbent. I continued my campaign efforts throughout the summer and fall, getting to know more people in my district and researching the current legislative issues. I won the general election in November with 70% of the vote. I was humbled with the trust the people of my home district had placed in me, and excited to represent them at the capitol. I was a somewhat nervous about the challenge ahead, until I read that the politicians who are most successful are those who have been tempered by the fires of adversity. After that, I felt confident that I had been well prepared for the job.

# Chapter 29

## Political Battlefield

When I first showed up as a volunteer aide in the legislature in 2015, there seemed to be an absence of leadership, and consequently an absence of a shared mental vision or mission. Having spent the last ten years of my life working with clearly defined goals in an organization with clearly spelled out articulated mission statements; I quickly became concerned that rudderless government was going nowhere fast. In 2017 as a newly elected representative, my concerns were confirmed, and even heightened. I noted that many people were hyper sensitive and cautious. Few people were willing to even acknowledge or discuss concerns about the missing leadership and shared vision.

Since I couldn't find clear direction anywhere in the capitol, I decided that I should begin by articulating the direction that I felt the legislature needed to be moving in. Just like when I'd "talk on" my fellow pilots to zero in on a target, I knew I needed to share my direction for the legislature. We needed to start with the broad vision of returning to the solid principles of our roots, so I looked to the US Constitution, the State Constitution, legislative rules, state laws, and honesty and morality. Surprisingly, these basic foundations were not a part of the common dialogue at the capitol. The few who dared to mention these were demeaned and insulted. Returning to the basics was not going to be an easy battle.

All of these are well-defined principles that have been agreed upon by an age-old process. They were carefully and solidly constructed but can still be modified if necessary, and they are meant to be good for everyone equally, yet, they were not welcome topics.

I have less faith in the system I encountered, as I learn more about the current state of our government. Foundational principles are being maneuvered, abused, and misused for the convenience of state agencies, powerful individuals, corporate interests, and a seemingly careful progression away from the original intent of our government. The legislative process is no longer trustworthy, and leadership is often unresponsive to requests for cooperation. They have devolved to dictating their will on the legislature, rather than building consensus.

Another major issue is media messaging. In many countries I visited overseas, government propaganda was shameless. Our media has been given great power by the First Amendment and were once the watchdogs that shielded us against corruption. They are now creeping steadily toward unprecedented bias, while federal and state government agencies have begun moving toward censorship of various media outlets, based on political affiliations.

As I work through the political process at the state level and engage with lobbyists and citizens of all types, I am reminded of a quote that I had to memorize during my Doolie year at the Academy. John Stuart Mill must have witnessed behavior similar to what we face today when he said:

> War is an ugly thing, but not the ugliest of things: the decayed and degraded state of moral and patriotic feeling which thinks that nothing is

worth a war, is much worse…A man who has nothing which he is willing to fight for, nothing which he cares more about than he does about his personal safety, is a miserable creature who has no chance of being free, unless made and kept so by the exertions of better men than himself.

One of the long-term goals I have conveyed through this book is my journey to develop leadership skills, strength, and character. I fully intend to use those skills to improve the political circumstances that my family and neighbors must live under.

> **The surprise is that we might become so used to that freedom that we could let them succeed.**

I have been committed to issues that are larger than myself my entire adult life, and this one is no different. I wholeheartedly believe that our American way of life is worth fighting for. The treasure of our hard-won freedom is one of the solid tenets in life that stands long after our material possessions have crumbled. There is no surprise that some might try to take it away from us for their own gain; the surprise is that we might become so used to that freedom that we could let them succeed.

I saw in Afghanistan that there are a lot of politics in war, and I had heard people describe politics as a battlefield. I didn't agree until I jumped into the political realm. Many of the political battles that were going on without the public's awareness didn't become apparent to me until I became an elected official, and it worries me that it seems to have been easy to keep the drastic changes being implemented in our government hidden from general public's knowledge.

One of the best and worst things about the military is that there are policies for everything. I firmly believe that good leadership is established on moral principles and processes, so that people don't have to live in fear of random, arbitrary mandates of the current political leader. In our country federal laws are based on and limited by the US Constitution; and the Idaho Constitution forms the basis for, and limits Idaho state laws. These are in place, so we don't have to live in fear of the arbitrary policy changes of a ruling class.

> I firmly believe that good leadership is established on moral principles and processes, so that people don't have to live in fear of random, arbitrary mandates.

Our Constitutional system is unique because it protects the people from government, which as history has shown, will often become more powerful and overbearing over time. When I arrived at the legislature, I witnessed our system beginning to be compromised. Our State Government agencies have manipulated the system to create policies that are not approved by state legislators, leaving the people out of the process, and our legislative leadership is beginning to marginalize the constitutional basis for, and limits of, state law.

I have seen what it looks like when the rule of law crumbles in a society and I have seen how effective and decisively an organization can work when based on law, direction and a shared vision. Just as when women try to conform to be a "man in a man's world" which contributes to the progression toward an unbalanced system, so conforming to the "political self-serving game" progresses a voracious system to propel and project itself for its own sake and not the sake of the people. I call on all leaders to stand strong with integrity, service, and excellence.

Curiously Strong

## Chapter 30

## *My Political Core Values*

When I competed in bench press competitions, it was the purity of the simple movement that drew me to it. Concise, clearly defined movements prove the true merit of a person's strength. An honest lift is beautiful and fluid, but a cheated lift bounces and jerks and is obvious to all watching. So too a life clearly defined by values is beautiful, and an organization racing towards a common goal is swift and sure.

> **My three core values that I use to guide my actions as an elected official every day: serve the people, work to maintain the republic, and cling to principle over power.**

I want to clearly define what I stand for, so that at any moment, my integrity as a legislator will be visible to all, and if I waiver, or stay true to my course, my constituents will always know. My principles are simple but concise and represent the values I was both born into and the values I have learned in service to my country. My three core values that I use to guide my actions as an elected official every day: serve the people, work to maintain the republic, and cling to principle over power.

### *Serve the People*

I ask myself how an unsustainable expanding government is able to gain traction and take more control each year. I believe the answer is in the strategies being used to hide the truth from the public.

Even if people within government have good intentions and are trying to do what they think is best for the "masses," they don't necessarily see the ripple effects of their actions on the people. Representatives are intended to be the voice of the people, not the voice of big government's unelected officials. I don't want to witness us throwing our freedoms and liberties away, only to then live in fear of our leaders, as do many of the people I encountered overseas.

> **Most of all, I believe elected officials should be servant leaders.**

I am contacted regularly by my constituents for many reasons, but I continue to be surprised by the number of letters I receive from citizens concerned about their freedom. Here is an excerpt from one of those letters: *"I am greatly concerned about the policies of our government. I do not worry for myself but for our children and grandchildren. Please help stop this insanity."*

I won't use this person's name, because most people who contact me do not want their names used. They are afraid of being subjected to some sort of retribution just for voicing their concerns. This is a terrible sign. This is how terrorism operates overseas, and those corrupt practices seem to be making inroads here too. I ask my constituents to allow me to use their stories without using their names, but some are not even comfortable doing that. Since Idaho is a state with a relatively small population, some people are concerned that by sharing their stories of their experiences, even without their name, someone will figure out who contacted me. They don't want their name out there. They are afraid of their government.

I do not want Americans to lose their freedoms or the representative form of government, and so I help constituents in my district with their disputes when the state is encroaching on their rights. I also help them navigate the cumbersome bureaucracy that has evolved from a huge system that is strangling individuals and businesses. The principles that support freedom and liberty need to be purposefully taught, and the rights of the people need to be defended; most of all, I believe elected officials should be servant leaders.

## *Maintain the Republic*

Part of maintaining the Republic rests in citizen involvement of the governmental process. Before the Roman Republic fell, its people were being entertained with free bread and circuses. It is my hope that Americans will recognize the importance of dedicating time toward keeping our Republic alive and well.

*I pledge allegiance to the flag of the United States of America, and to the Republic for which it stands, one Nation under God, indivisible, with liberty and justice for all.*

When I ponder the words of the Pledge of Allegiance, I rest on the word *Republic*. I imagine all the people who have given their lives for our Republic, and it saddens me that the ideals they fought for may be disappearing with little thought about the significance of our God-given rights and the protections provided by the Constitution.

In recent years America is more often referred to as a democracy than a republic. This is no small lapse. I was even shocked during a meeting when a Superintendent of Schools referred to our country as a democracy. If that is what schools are teaching our children now, it can be nothing less than intentional. The distinction between a democracy and a republic is important, as one is ever changing given the whims of the populace while the other is a constant based on principles and elections. It may be no coincidence that many schools throughout the country have stopped reciting the pledge of allegiance. If our country were in fact a democracy, it is not an exaggeration to say that America as we know it would no longer be free.

A pure democracy gives government authority directly to the will of the majority of the people. The danger of a democracy was exemplified by Greece and Rome, whose democracies failed to protect the rights of individuals who found themselves in the minority. In a democracy, the individual has no recourse but to obey the majority, the exact opposite intention of our founders and their major concern in individual freedom. Also in a democracy, although the people rule by majority, the citizens are granted privileges granted only by the government, known as civil rights. Furthermore, the morality is in constant flux as the people vote, generation to generation changing their minds. The rule of law is from the people. The people own the government and therefore the government "owns" the people. This is not freedom!

It was no small undertaking when the Founding Fathers put their efforts into forming a new government. At the center of their concern were the rights of the individual, which those rights would be protected no matter who was administering the government. This could only happen in a constitutional republic where the laws protect the people from the government.

America's unique greatness stems from its origins as a constitutional republic, one in which members of the government are democratically elected to represent the people. In our Republic, the founding principles are inextricably imbedded and framed by a constitution, which limits the infringement of the government on our rights. The rights do not come from government, but from inalienable God-given rights. These rights are not up for discussion. They cannot be altered by the people or by those governing and that is why the Constitution is the supreme law of the land.

The more dire threat to our republic is the ignorance of governmental actions that usurp authority from the people, and apathy towards the administration of the government. It is essential that citizenry, especially children, are educated to believe and participate in the process of our Republic; to understand the founding principles of our unique form of government; and to eagerly await the day when it is their turn to vote. I am very concerned at this time in history that many of the core principles of our country are being diluted, re-defined, and weakened.

To refer to America as a democracy is no small thing. It under-mines the primary principles of the Constitution, the representative republic and the rights of the individual to exercise freedom from a tyrannical government. This is why it is so important for Americans to come together to maintain the Republic and another reason why I am compelled to serve my country as an elected official.

## Power versus Principles

> **By far, the best leaders—the most effective ones—are those who value rock-solid principles over power.**

If my political legacy only leaves one mark on future generations, I hope that it is that I was a woman who stood in the face of adversity to uphold the principles of our great country.

The 21st century has brought the United States unique challenges. There are problems confronting Americans on many fronts, and I firmly believe that on each, we need principled leadership. Parents need to be principled leaders of their families. Principled leaders need to run our schools, teach our Sunday school classes, and run our volunteer organizations. They must encourage and listen, and when necessary, not be afraid to shed tears. Principled leaders must be able to think through complex, multi-level situations with compassion and practical common sense.

There are some sectors of our government organizations that operate based on principles, and there are some that are dominated by empire building, power hungry individuals and cliques. We need those who must interact with these power-dominated organizations to expose them and voice their demand for principle-based government.

By far, the best leaders—the most effective ones—are those who value rock-solid principles over power. When a leader is respected by his or her followers for characteristics they admire, the organization thrives and produces a quality result. While leadership is primarily a learned skill, it is undoubtedly affected by personal beliefs, values, ethics, character, and the desire to serve. Show me the beliefs, values and ethics associated with the person in charge and I will predict with accuracy the kind of leader a person aspires to be. Leadership cannot be separated from character; each is a reflection of the other.

Power is not to be confused with leadership. If a person arrives in a position of authority with the desire to rule, but not necessarily the desire to serve, an entirely new set of oppressive values, beliefs, and ethics will consistently emerge.

Principled leadership has many facets. Strengthening one's sense of purpose, character, connections, communication style, and focus are among them. I strive to continually improve these processes in my own life, and I want to encourage others to pursue them as well, because as a community we all benefit.

I started as a powerlifter and developed physical strength, continued as a fighter pilot and developed mental strength, and I hope to spend my career as a politician developing the strength of character needed to defend the principles of freedom and the rights of my neighbors. I hope that I always stand for sound moral principles. It is also vital that we pass these principles along to our succeeding generations, because in the words of Ronald Reagan:

> *"Freedom is never more than one generation away from extinction. We didn't pass it to our children in the bloodstream. It must be fought for, protected, and handed on for them to do the same."*

World Powerlifting Congress 1999 World Championships in Calgary, Alberta.

Soaring at the Air Force Academy during the summer of 2002.

81st Fighter Squadron at Spangdahlem Air Base, Germany in 2010.

M

C-12 crew members, 4th Expeditionary Reconnaissance Squadron, Bagram Airfield, Afghanistan in 2011.

Liberty Bell in front of the Idaho Capitol, 2016.

## *Afghanistan Air Medal Citation*

During my time in Afghanistan, I received a total of nine separate Air Medals for meritorious achievement in various combat operations. What follows is the citation from my fourth Air Medal, which I received after the events described in chapter 19, The Battle of Do Ab.

# THE UNITED STATES OF AMERICA

## TO ALL WHO SHALL SEE THESE PRESENTS, GREETING:
### THIS IS TO CERTIFY THAT
### THE PRESIDENT OF THE UNITED STATES OF AMERICA
### AUTHORIZED BY EXECUTIVE ORDER, MAY 11, 1942
### HAS AWARDED

## THE AIR MEDAL
### (FOURTH OAK LEAF CLUSTER)

### TO

**CAPTAIN PRISCILLA S. GIDDINGS**

### FOR
## MERITORIOUS ACHIEVEMENT
## WHILE PARTICIPATING IN AERIAL FLIGHT

Captain Priscilla S. Giddings distinguished herself by meritorious achievement while participating in sustained aerial flight as MC-12W Mission Commander, 4th Expeditionary Reconnaissance Squadron, 455th Expeditionary Operations Group, 455th Air Expeditionary Wing, Bagram Airfield, Afghanistan, from 24 May 2011 to 24 June 2011. During this period, Captain Giddings demonstrated superior airmanship and leadership while flying 20 high priority combat missions in support of Operation ENDURING FREEDOM. These sorties, executed day and night over hazardous terrain and under threat of hostile fire, provided coalition ground forces with critical Signals and Imagery Intelligence. As Air Warden, Captain Giddings deftly controlled air assets in support of six Helicopter Assault Forces which provided overwatch for 400 coalition forces, resulting in detainment of eight High Value Individuals. Additionally, she employed the MC-12W's multi-intelligence capabilities in locating 21 High Value Targets. Moreover, her rapid response to a Troops in Contact event ensured deconfliction of various aircraft in support of 64 ground forces surrounded and under fire from enemy insurgents. Her expertise helped prevent friendly casualties and resulted in 200 Enemy killed in action. Ultimately, her devotion to duty contributed to the stability of the Afghan government, the security of coalition ground forces and the safety of Afghan civilians. The professional ability and outstanding aerial accomplishments of Captain Giddings reflect great credit upon herself and the United States Air Force.

**GIVEN UNDER MY HAND**

**11 APRIL 2012**

**DAVID L. GOLDFEIN**
**Lieutenant General, USAF**
**Commander, USAFCENT**

# *Bibliography*

(1) Adapted from Webster's New Twentieth Century Dictionary, 2nd edition, 1983

(2) Adapted from Webster's New Twentieth Century Dictionary, 2nd edition, 1983

(3) Adapted from Webster's New Twentieth Century Dictionary, 2nd edition, 1983

## *Acknowledgements*

This book would not have been possible without encouragement from Women Ignite International, an organization of leaders who are driven to help women succeed professionally and personally. Their publishing team provided the support needed for the completion of this book.

Leadership Development Press got me started actually writing the book and provided many good ideas.

A life-long friend from the Academy, Dominique Snedeker, shared her expertise in English during the final rewrites of this book. I am greatly indebted to Dominique's friendship and hard work in bringing this manuscript to completion.

Kristen Mehraban is a friend and local Idaho artist who provided the hand drawn artwork. I hope her artwork will continue to inspire women throughout Idaho and the world.

My husband and my mother both spent many hours proofreading, editing and making suggestions.

My friend Martha Falk, my father, siblings, and coworkers all gave steadfast support, encouragement, and assistance— thank you.

Most importantly, I must give my utmost thanks to God for allowing me to experience the opportunities that shaped my life, and the opportunity to share my story with young women who might benefit from it.

## *About the Author*

Priscilla Giddings was raised on a small, family ranch in White Bird, Idaho and graduated from Salmon River High School in Riggins where she was the valedictorian and student body president. A four-sport athlete in high school, she was recruited for the track and field program at the Air Force Academy where she graduated with a Bachelor of Science degree in Biology.

After college she attended pilot training and went on to be selected to fly a fighter aircraft, the A-10 Warthog. Upon completing fighter training at Davis-Monthan Air Force Base, she was the only one in her class to be awarded "Top Gun," a weapons employment precision award. She followed her A-10 assignment with a career-broadening assignment flying as the mission commander on intelligence, surveillance and reconnaissance (ISR) missions in the MC-12.

Priscilla deployed in support of Operation Enduring Freedom three times. She has flown gliders, C-182s, DA-20s, T-6s, T-38s, A-10s, and MC-12s and has logged a thousand combat hours and was awarded nine air medals. While serving overseas, she was able to continue her education and complete a Master of Science in Physiology from the California University of Pennsylvania.

She separated from active duty in July 2014 and joined the Idaho Air National Guard as an Air Liaison Officer for the 124th Air Support Operations Squadron. She currently serves in the Air Force Reserves as the Director of Idaho Admissions Liaisons for the Air Force Academy and ROTC.

After separating from active duty, Priscilla set about defending freedom through local government. She was elected in 2016 to the Idaho House of Representatives for District 7A. She represents 45,000 Idahoans covering 18,000 square miles of land.

She lives on a small ranch in central Idaho with her family. She continues to travel across the country as a motivational speaker highlighting the importance of "Strong Women."

*This book is proudly published by WIPublish,*
*A Division of Women Ignite International.*

Contact: Terilee Harrison, Director WIPublish
terilee@womenigniteinternational.com

Find us online: www.womenigniteinternational.com
LIKE us on Facebook: www.Facebook.com/wipublish

59965099R00120

Made in the USA
Columbia, SC
11 June 2019